ALCATRAZ

Marvin E Coon
#1422
1959—1963

ALCATRAZ

The True End of the Line

An Autobiography
of the Life and Times of Former Inmate
DARWIN COON

New Desmas Press
Sacramento

Published by
New Desmas Press
1805 Tribute Road, Suite H,
Sacramento, California 95815
NewDesmasPress@aol.com
Cover photo by P.R. Severaid

ISBN-10: 0-9679592-2-5
ISBN-13: 978-0-9679592-2-1

Printed in the United States of America

I would like to dedicate this book to my sister

Harriet Jean Ralston

for her support and help in all aspects of my pursuits in writing this book.

CONTENTS

My Little Boy

Once he was my baby boy
I held his tiny hands
And helped him
Through his toddlin' day
As he grew up to be a man
I'd kiss the bumps he got each day
And love his curly head
I'd rock him off to slumber land
And tuck him in his bed
I'd told him bedtime stories
Of the little bears
I'd even told him stories
Of the golden stairs
I taught about the Bible
And the straight and narrow way
But somewhere on the road of life
He turned and went astray
Now it's too late for mother
To help her a'wanderin' son
She cannot reach those hands
Nor can she guide those feet
For he is in prison
Where mother cannot reach
But mother keeps on praying
Yes praying night and day
That God will go through those gray walls
And ease his troubled heart
And bring him back to this cold world
A man to do his part

By Florence Coon 1958

PREFACE

An incorrigible person is a threat to the citizens of the United States of America. I had realized that all I wanted to do was serve my time and become a productive citizen. That is to me a great problem in the prison system of this country. A person gets a sentence and there is no escape from that sentence. No matter how much that prisoner would like to give up and say, *Ok, you win, I surrender,* a prisoner has no place to give up. If there was some way to determine when a prisoner reached that point, a lot of money could be saved and that inmate could be returned to the free world to become a productive citizen.

Alcatraz was considered the last resort. When the authorities of the federal prison system made the decision that an inmate should be housed at Alcatraz, they had made that decision based on the past conduct of that inmate. The inmate in question was considered to be an incorrigible person and would probably spend the rest of his life in prison. Of course this is a falsehood, because no one can determine what any individual will do from day to day or from year to year for that matter. I'm an example of that very fact. I was released in 1972 after being in numerous prisons and spending most of my prime years behind bars. I have done nothing unlawful since. To me, this proves that anyone can change. You should never prejudge anyone because of the situation that person is in.

People are very curious about what went on inside Alcatraz when it was open and operating. There were some truly terrible things that took place on that little island in San Francisco Bay. One of the most historic events that took place while I was housed there was the attempted escape by Frankie Morris and by John and Clarence Anglin.

Alcatraz was the true end of the line. When the federal prison system sent you there, you were considered by them to be beyond redemption. I was sent to Alcatraz from the federal penitentiary at Leavenworth, Kansas in 1959. I spent four years of my life on the island of Alcatraz and I was one of the last group of men to leave it when it was closed in 1963.

INTRODUCTION

Concerns of a Prison Inmate

There are always three things that are on the mind of a man serving time in prison. I guess I should re-phrase that and say that there were three things constantly on my mind! My number one concern was staying alive. Number two was to keep from going crazy, and number three was my struggle to keep away from being homosexually assaulted by other inmates.

Prison is such an unnatural environment and there are always those inmates who really don't care what happens. They are always looking for some way to cause problems. They will agitate others into riots, fighting, etc. and when the chaos starts, they will slip away into the background, so as not to be seen as directly involved. It is really surprising how many such characters like that there are in prisons. Of course, these types of people **do** get involved many times because sooner or later the other inmates figure out how they are being manipulated and many of the offenders wind up dead.

There are many things that can cause problems inside a prison. Gambling causes a lot of trouble between inmates. There is a lot of betting carried on inside, especially on sporting events. When it comes time to pay up, and the loser can't, or won't pay, then there is serious trouble. The same thing happens when one inmate borrows something from another one and neglects to replace it.

However, if you were to ask anyone who has served time, what it is that causes the most friction, ninety-nine out of a hundred will tell you that the answer is homosexuality. I don't think that they keep records, but I would say that 90 per cent of all killings inside prisons are connected with it.

One inmate stealing another's goods is also a frequent source of conflict. If you witness a break-in, it's your duty as a *stand-up con* to inform the inmate who had his belongings stolen, who did it. Of course, sometimes this will result in a very big problem for an innocent person. If an inmate should have it in for another, he will tell the inmate whose stuff was taken, that *Joe Blow* was the offender when he really wasn't. Unfortunately, there is a lot of this type of thing and oftentimes the wrong inmate will get beaten up or even killed over something that he didn't do. Prison is a big powder keg and you never know when someone will light the fuse. You have to be constantly aware of everything that is going on around you, or you could wind up getting released early by going out the back gate in a pine box.

1

Iowa Training School for Boys

It was a day in late September and the blue waters of San Francisco Bay sparkled merrily in the warm rays of the sun. From the slatted wooden deck of the prison boat, the venerable Warden Johnson, I felt anything but merry though as I gazed wistfully back to watch the skyline of that famous Baghdad-like city fall away, marking the ends of the earth where I had just dropped off. Shackled in leg-irons to a half-dozen other men, I was dirty and weary from my long train ride out of Wichita, Kansas. I pulled the last long drag out of my

Marlborough Red and flicked the stub into a passing wave. I was headed to Alcatraz, to become forever, along with a thousand other men, and more, a part of The Rock. It was autumn, 1959 and I was twenty-six years old.

Still chained together, we were debarked and unceremoniously herded into an old yellow school-bus, and as it crept, laboring and protesting up the serpentine slope that led to the front of the dreaded prison, I wondered what would happen to us if the brakes suddenly gave way. On our right-hand side, there were but inches to where the steep granite cliffs fell away into the churning waters below. Out in the Bay, near a mass of land that I later learned was Angel Island, a few delta shaped sail-boats bobbed brightly about. Further to the right of them, I could just make out the graceful arch of the famous Golden Gate bridge, half-hidden in a thick cloud of morning fog.

When the bus finally negotiated the last hairpin curve and came squealing to a rolling stop, I was relieved, to say the least. We were quickly marched out and made to shuffle over and form a line facing several uniformed guards who were standing on a portico in front of the solid steel doors that framed the front of the main building. The salt air was crisper and damper up here than it had been down on the dock. The chill permeated my thin cotton jumpsuit and I shivered involuntarily. Directly opposite the prison doors the jagged outline of the city of San Francisco

2

loomed shockingly close, so near it seemed that I could reach out my hand and touch it, yet so far, that it may as well have been on the moon. A seagull wheeled restlessly overhead, its raucous calls of freedom mingling incongruously with the sounds of feet and chains scuffling on cement.

Next, as a group we were ushered through the massive front doors of the main cell house. First the electric lock buzzed to open them, then as they slammed shut behind us, we had to wait as a key was lowered down so that an officer could unlock a barred gate in front of us. We were then led into a long narrow room where the leg-irons and hand-cuffs were finally snapped off. Since we had worn them since leaving Leavenworth several days ago, every one of us had sore swollen wrists and ankles and we were overjoyed to be free of them. Then, in turn, each of us was ordered to undress completely, and one by one, we were subjected to a very thorough strip search. Lastly, we were paraded naked, to the hoots and cat-calls of the inmates, down the long corridor of triple-decked cells that would come to be our home and that we came to know as *Broadway*.

Just short of the dining hall, we were escorted down a short flight of metal stairs to where the showers were. The shower room was an enormous open area. A guard could stand in the middle of the room and see activity anywhere. Each of us was given a tiny bar of industrial strength soap and the guards watched as we attempted to scrub off the stink of the long train ride from Kansas. I was somewhat shocked to find that the water was cold, but just being given a chance to be clean again had become a luxury that I no longer took for granted.

Reflecting back on my life, it almost seems that I was destined for a place like Alcatraz from the very first. On a cold winter's day in January, 1933, I was born in my parents' modest home where my mother was alone, except for my father's sister Jenny. My father had gone into the tiny mid-western town of Anthon, Iowa, to get the doctor. Just as they returned, I came into this world, struggling and fighting to breathe, all ten pounds, twelve ounces of me.

"Goodness," the doctor exclaimed. "We should just put some overalls on him and send him out to play!"

Anthon was at that time, much as it is now, a small farming hamlet of about five hundred people. It lies in the northwest corner of Iowa, not far from Sioux City, an area that after the Civil War became home to a diverse population of immigrants. Among them were Germans, Swedes, Norwegians, Danes, Dutch, Croatians, Italians and African-Americans. Some of them were drawn to the lush green land for farming while others first sought work in the coal mines of central and southern Iowa before migrating farther north.

Small quantities of coal were first mined in the 1840's near Fort Des Moines and from shallow seams along the lower Des Moines River. Coal-fired steamboats were starting to appear on America's newly opened waterways and these beds of energy were a fortuitous discovery. By 1876, Iowa was the leading coal producing area west of the Mississippi, and fifth overall in the United States. Steam locomotives also required huge amounts of coal and as the mining industry grew, so did the ever expanding network of rail lines. With more railroads of course, came more people and greater settlement of the American west.

The first known Europeans to venture into Iowa territory were the French explorers Louis Joliet and Father Jacques Marquette, a Jesuit missionary. They and their party traveled down the Mississippi and came ashore in 1673. The gently rolling hills and the dark rich soil, so inducive to good farming, awed them at once. At that time, seventeen different Native American tribes inhabited the area. These included the Sauk, the Iowa, the Mesquakie, the Sioux, the Potawami, the Otoe and the Missouri. Iowa is still home to the Mesquakie tribe and there is a big reservation still, near Anthon. When I was a boy, I often spent many a carefree summer afternoon down at the river playing with my friend Chuck Raymond, a full-blooded Sioux Indian.

My family settled in northwest Iowa in the middle 1800's. They were farming people, having come west to the Blackhawk State from West Virginia, Ohio and Indiana. My mother used to always tell us that we were descended from the Pennsylvania Dutch, and indeed there is a record of a Philip Coon who along with two of his brothers, immigrated to Philadelphia in 1720. They were originally Mennonites from Holland and of Walloon ancestry, which means that they had Celtic roots. Coon is but one variation on a family name that can be spelled *Coons, Koon, Kuhn, Kuntz,* and so on.

The brothers eventually went their separate ways, and Philip, along with his rather large family, settled in what is now Marion County, West Virginia, where they built Coon's Fort in the 1770's. The Coon family had members who fought in the French and Indian Wars as well as in the War of Independence. Since my grandfather had French Canadian and Indian blood, it is likely that I am descended from some hardy soul who migrated even farther north, perhaps to trap furs in the Canadian wilderness, However, there are so many descendants of the original three brothers, and so many that were lost track of, that today it is impossible to trace the genealogy precisely. My other grandfather on my mother's side was a Luce and he came west from Missouri in a Conestoga wagon

Those early settlers found that wood for building homes was scarce in some parts of Iowa, especially on the prairie, so for fuel they resorted to using the materials that were available, dried prairie hay and corncobs. Winters could be harsh and unforgivingly cold. To survive, the newcomers often had to follow the example of the native Indians and construct dwellings out of sod.

Anthon's nickname also mirrored its White and Native American ancestry. Known humorously by the locals as *Animal Town,* it was virtually impossible when I was growing up to do business with anyone who did not have some sort of animal as a last name. My father was but one of twelve Coon children living and farming in the region. Our next door neighbor, Harry Fox, ran the only garage and car dealership in town. Andy Wolf and his family owned the lumberyard while the Beaver family were plumbers. The movie theater was owned and operated by the Lions, while Clarence Mink supplied fuel to the farmers from his twin gas stations. Mary Bird was the retired schoolteacher who gave piano lessons, and if you patronized either of the two cafés you would likely be served by a member of the Rabbit family. Finally, on your last trip out of town to the local boot hill, you would be in the care of the town undertaker, Frank Colt.

The Depression years of the 1930's and my early upbringing formed much of my character and was to contribute to my ensuing unhappiness and eventual acting out. I was the youngest and the fourth child of the family, with two older sisters and one brother. In those days, everyone in the community experienced the pinch of economic hard times but in the Coon clan, we did encounter suffering. Early on, my father had rejected the farming life and taking his portion of the inheritance from the land, he had bought a small wooden house in Anthon where he found work as a railroad worker. He was also known to make and sell a little home brew.

The house quickly became much too inadequate for a growing family and as work grew scarce, my father was forced to move from job to job. Oftentimes, there wasn't much to eat on the table. We had no electricity and no indoor plumbing, although we did have running water in the kitchen. The bathroom was an outhouse quite a few yards from the back door and my brother and I often used to see who could set the fastest record using it on cold winter days.

My mother doted on me, her baby boy, and by the time that I was old enough to go to school, I was a little terror. I was used to always having my own way at home and I had subsequently developed a terrible temper. My tantrums were legendary in the family. It didn't help that I quickly became aware that I was the smallest boy in my class, indeed in the whole school, and when the other kids started picking on me and calling me *Shorty* I was frequently infuriated and in a constant state of barely repressed rage. It erupted one day when the teacher tried to discipline me over some small thing and like a wild animal suddenly unleashed, I flew at her and bit her in the leg, hard enough to draw blood. As she fought me off, screaming, I stabbed her in the arm with an ink pen. My father didn't say a word to me when he finally got me home and settled down; perhaps he was too shocked, or perhaps he had warned my overly-indulgent mother that this day would come. At any rate, it was she who had to deal with me, which she did, to her credit, and after that I didn't cause any more trouble at school until I was much older.

My father did what he could to help my situation

though, intervening in his own quiet and well-meaning way. There was one big overgrown bully in school who made it his life's mission to lie in wait for me every day after class, and chase me home. I was terrified of him. One afternoon, as he pursued me past the grain elevators where my father happened to be working at the time, I heard my Dad's voice shout at us. I stopped running and the other boy stopped too and then walked off in the opposite direction. My father came over and asked me why I was running. I told him the truth, that I was afraid of getting beat up.

"I'm ashamed of you," he thundered, and as he had never spanked me or even spoken to me in a harsh tone before, his disapproval cut me to the quick. He pressed his big hand to my shoulder and squeezed so hard that I winced in pain.

"You go catch that kid and stand up to him or I'll give you a good whipping myself!"

I knew that he meant it or he wouldn't have said it. I reluctantly started back up the dusty road in an effort to overtake my tormentor. Each step that I took, I just knew that it was about to become my last. When the bully heard me behind him, he spun around on his heel and I could see by his eyes that he was astonished to see me. I didn't give him any time to think though, and I just tore into him, much as I had the unlucky first-grade teacher. I felt a great sense of satisfaction as I smacked him square on the nose and he began bleeding. The next thing I knew, he was the one in tears fleeing, his hands held up to cup his injured face. I didn't chase after him but walked slowly back to where my father was waiting. I was somewhat amazed at myself and savoring this newly-found sense of empowerment.

"That's good, son, " my Dad said, drawing me close to him. "Now don't go looking for trouble, but don't let me catch you running away from it either!"

It was a lesson in manly behavior that I never forgot and that was to serve me well in later years.

In the early 1940's when the second World War broke out, every able-bodied person began looking for a job in the war factories. My father, like a lot of other people, thought it best to follow the work, so he sold the family house for a few thousand dollars, and moved his brood to Sioux City, where prosperity beckoned. There were just two of us children at home now, as my oldest sister had married and my brother had joined the navy. Less than a year later, my world turned upside down. My parents separated and my mother moved out of the house, although she did stay in Sioux City.

I couldn't understand how she could just leave us like that and I really missed her warmth and presence in our home. It was at this time that my famous temper returned. I began to act out more and more, giving in to my impulses. It didn't help that my father was working the night shift and sleeping days. Along with my sister Harriet, who was three years older, I was suddenly left

Darwin, age 12, playing with a pal.

pretty much on my own. We had to learn to take care of ourselves. As might be expected, it wasn't long before I was getting into serious trouble.

Soon, I started staying out late at night and running around with kids older than I was. I was always getting caught by the police for being out after curfew. The first few times they took me to the police station and kept me overnight. My father would come and get me and give me a talking to. Most of the cops came to know me and they would try to talk to me too, and then take me home. None of what they said ever sunk in. I would just go out and do it again. Then my father decided to move closer to his job and the neighborhood that we moved into was not quite as nice as the one we left.

I found new friends and started running around again at night. I also started playing hookey from school. School for the most part, was always very easy for me. I would finish my lesson before the rest of the kids and somehow wind up in trouble with the teacher. I was often bored with school. When I played hookey I would go down to the river and fish. Of course, the school would get in touch with my father and he would have to give me a talking to. He would tell me, "You have to go to school or they are going to send you to the reform school at Eldora! You have to go to school! There is nothing I can do for you. If you don't go to school, they are going to send you away!"

My sister, who attended another school, would even walk me to the front door. I would go in the front and right out the back and head for the river. The authorities did give me numerous chances to straighten myself out and attend classes on a regular basis. I would go for a few days and then I'd be right back down at the river. Then one day, like my father had warned me, the police picked me up and took me to the county jail. The law said that I

Darwin at 12 years old. Photo taken at Iowa Training School for Boys.

had to go to school until I finished the eighth grade or turned sixteen.

In Juvenile Court the judge sentenced me to an undetermined time at the Iowa Training School for Boys, located in Eldora. On the way there, the officer stopped for lunch. Upon exiting the coffee shop, I took off and got away from him. I had no idea where I was or where I was going to go. I walked along a dirt road until I was really tired and it was getting dark. I tucked myself away in a

Darwin, 14 years old at Iowa Training School for Boys.

cornfield and laid down. I fell asleep right away and I slept all night. I woke up in the morning with the sun shining on me. Boy, was I hungry!

Out on the road once again, I managed to finally hitch a ride with a farmer. He took me to his farm and fed me a big meal. He gave me a dollar and told me to stay on the highway, that it would take me to Sioux City. I caught another ride and this time I got as far as Solon, Iowa. I was now only eight miles from home. A cattle truck stopped for me and took me the rest of the way into the city.

I didn't dare go home because I knew that my father hadn't yet gone to work, so I went down into the storm drains that ran under the streets and waited until the coast was clear. Then I went home and changed into clean clothes. I was starving, so I raided the ice box. I was by then so exhausted that I laid down on my bed and fell fast asleep.

When my father returned, he shook me awake and persuaded me to go down to the police station and turn myself in. I told him that I would and then I left the house. I had gone only a block when the police spotted me and took me to the station. The next morning I was on my way back to Eldora, but this time it was a little different. The officer put shackles on my ankles and said, "You won't outrun me this time!"

I had heard about Eldora from some of the kids that I ran around with, so I knew what to expect. When we got there, the officer handed me over to the Dean of Boys. He took me to his office and explained to me what would happen if I tried to escape. Then he took me over to the hospital building and locked me in a room. He said that after some tests I'd be moved to the little boys' cottage which was for boys twelve and under.

Eldora was like a military school. We wore uniforms at dress occasions such as meals, church, visiting days and dress parade. We were required to work an assigned job for one-half of the day and to attend school the other half. We were required to march everywhere we went. We lived in a dormitory under the supervision of a husband and wife team known as *cottage parents*. We were assigned a cottage according to our age. The cottages ranged from twelve and under up to the age of twenty-one.

Each cottage had a captain and a sergeant. Rank was determined by how good we were with our fists. If we wanted to, we could challenge the sergeant for his cap. If we defeated the sergeant, we could challenge the captain. If someone whipped the captain, then he became the captain of his cottage. The tougher you were, the higher your rank.

Life at Eldora was a game of wits between the cottage parents and the inmates. The main goal of the inmates was *to beat the man*. To beat the man was to do anything and everything possible without the man catching you. If you did something against the rules and were caught, it became the captain's job to discipline you and keep you in line.

After a few days, I decided to run away. One morning as we were lining up for breakfast, I hit the cornfield.

There were no fences around the place so it wasn't hard to take off. What I didn't know was how well they knew all the roads and fields. Some of them just went to the first road and waited for me to come out and then they had me. I was truly surprised to see them standing there watching for me.

Unfortunately, I also did not know that there was a set punishment for running away. The punishment was ten licks from the man in charge of the guardhouse, as it was called, three days in *the hole* and twenty-seven more days on the coal pile. The ten licks from the strap were not very pleasant. The strap was a strip of leather with holes in it. When you got hit you really felt it. They had what was called *the strapping pole.* It had a hook about eye level and they would tie your hands and put them over the hook.

They tied me to the pole and told me that I had to thank the man each time he hit me. He struck me the first time and I said, "Thank you, sir." He replied in a very gruff voice that that one didn't count. I also had to count each one off and then thank him. He hit me again and I said, "One, thank you, sir!" After a few of these, I became so mad that I lost my temper and started calling that man every bad name that I could think of. Of course, that was just what he wanted me to do, and he started hitting me harder and faster until he wore himself completely out.

Afterwards they took me to the hole and it was just that. The door was so small that I had to get down on my hands and knees to crawl inside. I was helped along from a big boot in my rear. I had a very sore backside and the backs of my legs turned blue from the strapping. I was given only bread and water twice a day for the next three days. The following twenty-seven weren't much fun either. The inmates in punishment got all of the dirty jobs that they could find. Every morning we loaded the truck with empty garbage cans and went to the kitchen to pick up the garbage from the day before. After emptying the cans, we had to really scrub them so they would be ready for the next day.

Then if there was coal to be unloaded, we were sent to the coal pile. If there was no coal, we were sent to the dairy barn to clean the stalls. When we finally got back to our quarters in the guardhouse, we had to sit on the concrete floor and await our turn for a shower. Then back to the concrete until they called your name for chow. After chow, it was the same until bedtime. Needless to say, I was very happy to get back to my cottage.

When it got close to my birthday, I tried to be on my best behavior. The day after my birthday, I was moved to another cottage. I was there only a few days when I got into a fight with the sergeant. One of the inmates encouraged me to challenge the boy for his cap. I thought about it and decided that it was a good idea as the sergeants and captains got special treatment and privileges that the others did not. After supper, I went up to the sergeant and said, "I want your cap." He went and got the captain and the three of us went into the locker room. I got a few bruises but I won the cap. Then it was the captain's turn. He wasn't expecting the challenge and for the next three nights after the evening meal we went to the locker room and had a go at it. I couldn't whip him and he couldn't whip me. The fourth night he gave up and became my sergeant. I was ecstatic! No one was brave enough to challenge either one of us after that and we made a good team.

Seeing I was captain now, I decided to change a few things. When the cottage parents told us to take an inmate to the locker room and discipline him, we'd play *beat the man*. We'd tell him to holler while we yelled and banged on the lockers. Sometimes we'd tear his shirt just to make it look good. Later we would sit back and have a good laugh at how we had out-foxed them.

After thirteen months I was paroled to the custody of my mother. I was home for several months and then I was arrested for breaking into a house and stealing property. I was promptly sent back to Eldora. Now it was the summer of 1946 and no school classes were being held so we were assigned to work in harvesting. I went to work in the cannery. One day I was grinding up green tomatoes to make pickle relish. I was fooling around and I got careless. I got my right hand caught in the grinding machine and it cut off the first joint of three of my fingers. After a few days in the hospital I was assigned to work in the front office as a runner. Afraid that my parents would sue them, the administration decided to release me again to the custody of my mother.

Just nine days before my release date, a terrible event occurred. One of the inmates in the guardhouse was subjected to a vicious beating while working on the coal pile. He was taken to the hospital where later that night he died. When word got out that morning, we rioted and took over the institution. All of the staff fled and we had free run of the place. A lot of the inmates took advantage of the situation and ran away.

As I was only days away from being released, I stayed as did quite a few others. We went into the living quarters of the cottage parents and helped ourselves to cigarettes and liquor. There was plenty of food in the kitchen and bakery so we just enjoyed ourselves and waited to see what would happen. The National Guard came in and took control of the situation after a day or so. A lot of the employees were fired from their jobs. The man who beat the boy to death was arrested and eventually convicted of manslaughter and sent to prison.

The State of Iowa changed everything at the institution after that. All of the staff were replaced and the facility was no longer run in a military fashion. There were no more fist fights to determine captains and sergeants. Boys over eighteen were sent to a different facility. I was finally released and I went to live with my mother and her new man in South Sioux City, Nebraska, just across the river from Sioux City, Iowa.

The California
Youth Authority

I had found out that breaking into houses was not as profitable as I had thought. Now I started breaking into stores and business places. I began my new career by hanging around the used car lot and garage that belonged to the man with whom my mother was living. I thought that he was a pretty nice guy. He started sending me to the parts stores for car parts. I knew how to drive but I didn't have a driver's license. Every time that I went across the bridge into Iowa, I was afraid that a cop would stop me and send me back to Eldora.

Darwin E. Coon's graduation picture—17 years old.

I finally got my license, but one day as I was looking for a car part in one of the stores I noticed a truck parked at the back. It was loaded with brand new whitewall tires. The war had ended, but tires were still very hard to come by. I found a buddy of mine and we began discussing ways of stealing the whole truckload. We knew of a deserted farm with a big barn on it. We decided that we could hide the truck out there while we found a buyer for the tires.

After dark, we went to look the place over. There were alarms on all the doors and windows. We made our way up to the roof. There was a skylight with no alarm that we could see, so we got some tools and a very long heavy rope. After carefully removing one of the glass panes, my friend dropped a part of the rope down into the building. Then he crawled through the open pane and grabbed a hold of the rope to lower himself down. Only thing was, in our eagerness to break in, neither one of us had thought to tie the rope off! He fell in a sickening heap to the concrete floor below.

There was blood all over his legs so I knew that he was hurt pretty badly. There was still a portion of the rope on the roof, so I tied it off and let myself down to where he was. One of his legs was broken and the bone was sticking right out through the skin. I got him into the truck and quickly hit every switch on the panel until the door opened. We had parked his car behind the local school house, so that's where we took the truck and left it.

On the way to the hospital we cooked up the story that we were goofing around and he fell off of the War Eagle Monument. That was something forbidden that boys did all the time. After I left him at the hospital, I went back and drove the truck and the tires out to the barn. We had left my car there earlier in the evening and

I drove back to the hospital in it. My buddy was fine and his mother was there with him.

Another buddy steered me to a guy who dealt in stolen goods. I told him that I had fifty new whitewall tires for sale and he offered me one thousand dollars, take it or leave it. I took it. That night I drove the truck to the assigned spot and collected the money. A few days later I saw the man in a bar and he told me that he had sold some of the tires to the police department. I gave my partner in the hospital his half of the take and we had a good laugh over that.

Shortly afterwards, my mother and her boyfriend decided to move to California and my mother asked me to come along. We moved to Oakland, and in just a short time I fell in with a couple of brothers who were in the armed robbery business. I was in the Golden State for just a few months when I got arrested two times for armed robbery. Both times I had a jury trial and I was found *not guilty*. I decided to slow down and take it easy for awhile. However, the two brothers had other ideas. They needed a third man for a job that they had planned. Well, during the job, everything went wrong! One of the brothers was shot and the other two of us were caught and arrested. This time the jury found us *guilty*. I was sent to the California Youth Authority at their facility in Lancaster. Boy, what a nightmare that was! Lancaster was located right in the middle of the desert.

The housing there consisted of barracks with double

bunks and no air-conditioning, which made life miserable. Plus, the inmates ran in gangs and there was continuous trouble between the gangs all of the time. There were four white gangs, one Mexican and one African-American one. They all fought against each other, even the white ones as they were from different cities—LA, Oakland, San Francisco and San Diego.

Our personal belongings were kept in metal lockers next to our bunks. There were constant break-ins and almost always there was a witness to the theft. Afterwards, a big fight always ensued and most of the time there were pipes and homemade knives involved. Someone always got hurt really badly and oftentimes someone was killed.

Like at all prisons, the goal here was *to beat the man.* At Lancaster they didn't have the means available to lock down the prison in a maximum way. The inmates took advantage of that because there was no way to separate more than ten inmates at a time from the general population. The inmates tried all they could to disrupt the flow of prison life and the boredom of everyday routine, even going so far as to set fire to the barracks. When the firemen turned out, the inmates would shower them with rocks or whatever they could find, some of it not too pleasant. Lancaster had a vocational program with shops located in an old airplane hangar. There were numerous trades to learn, but the only things that I ever saw produced were homemade knives

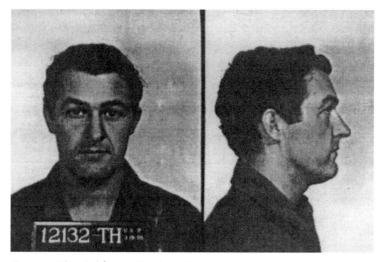

Coon at The California Youth Authority.

and weapons in preparation for the next melee. All of us lived in constant fear of what would happen next.

I spent thirteen months at Lancaster before being moved to new facilities at Tracy for my remaining two months of incarceration. After my release I decided that I would look up some of the new friends that I had made in those two places. I took a trip to LA and met up with a couple of guys who had worked in the print shop at Lancaster. Now they had their very own printing business. Of course, theirs wasn't exactly on the up-and-up! They had studied photo-engraving while serving time. It didn't take them long to put into practice all that they had learned! They were busy printing fake I.D.s and were photo-engraving American Express cheques.

They agreed to front me $5,000.00 in cheques. After I cashed them, they said that they would sell me all that I wanted for $10.00 per thousand. Well, I papered Southern California. The cheques were really good quality and very easy to cash. I went back and bought $50,000.00 worth and went on the road cashing them in. I would go into a clothing store and buy a very nice shirt and pay for it with one of the phoney cheques which was worth a hundred dollars. At another store I might buy a pair of good slacks or some shoes. I'd go into a grocery store and get a couple of cartons of cigarettes.

At night I would stop at a motel or hotel, always one that had a bar. I'd register at the desk and then go to the bar. I'd have a couple of drinks and then cash one of the phoney cheques. The next morning I would check out and pay with another one. I'd move on down the road and do the same thing all over again. I was leaving a paper trail across the country which unbeknowst to me, the FBI was following.

When I got home to Sioux City, I found some of my old pals and we lived it up pretty good, just partying and hanging out at bars. However, I stayed too long in Sioux City. After about a week, the police found me in a bar. When they searched my car, they found the cheques. I was charged with interstate transportation of forged securities. I pled *guilty* in federal court and the judge sentenced me to five years. I was taken to the federal penitentiary at Terra Haute, Indiana but I was there for only ten days. Because of my age, I was transferred to the federal reformatory at El Reno, Oklahoma, where the inmates were between the ages of 18–25.

Federal Reformatory, El Reno, Oklahoma

I consider El Reno as the worst prison that I was ever in. At that time, prisoners were actually buying and selling other inmates. That may sound unreal but it really did happen. When a new inmate arrived there, they put him in what was called A&O, Admission & Orientation. Most new inmates spent about thirty days in A&O. That period was intended for the inmate to get adjusted to prison routine. Also, it gave him time to learn the rules. They also were put through a testing period so

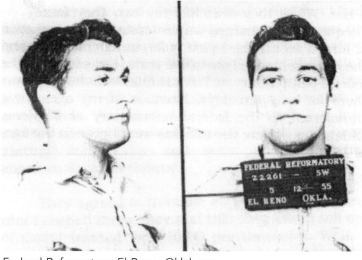

Federal Reformatory, El Reno, Oklahoma.

that the authorities could determine where that particular inmate would work while serving his sentence.

El Reno inmates, like those in many prisons, run in gangs and where there are gangs, there is always trouble. The administrations of prisons know about the gangs but there is very little that they can do about them. When new inmates hit the general population, gang members single them out. If you don't stand up for yourself, you become the property of a gang. The gang will take all of your personal property and they will sexually assault you. The only way out is to fight for yourself against four or five gang members. The correctional officers will get involved only if there is a fight. Then they hustle everybody down to the *TU*, the Treatment Unit, which is solitary imprisonment, and the next morning they usher you before the disciplinary committee.

When the gang members approach a new inmate, they ask the question, "Who is taking care of you?" If the new inmate says, " No one," which is the most common answer, he is told, " In that case you belong to us". Then one of two things happen: either there is a fight or the gang takes everything the new prisoner has, including his body. If someone wants an inmate that belongs to a gang all you have to do is go to the leader and ask to buy that man. The gang leader will set a price, with the usual price being 25 cartons of cigarettes or the same amount in other commissary items. At the time I was in El Reno, cigarettes sold for about $2.30 per carton, which came to about $57.50 for the price of a man.

To me, that seemed very unnatural, but first let me relate what happened the first day that I hit the general population. I knew a couple of guys that I had served time with in California. They had sent me a *kite* (note) while I was in A&O. The note explained what would take place the day that I hit the general population, so fortunately, I knew ahead of time what to expect.

I was lying on my bunk when the whistle blew, releasing all of the work crews. The inmates started coming in from their work assignments, and sure enough, here came four inmates. They surrounded my bunk, but I already knew what was coming. One of the four said to me,

"Who's taking care of you?" I said back to him in as calm a voice as I could, "Darwin Coon."

You should have seen the look on that inmate's face! He sort of scratched his head and said, "Who is Darwin Coon?" I said back to him, "That's me, Buddy!" At that very moment I stood up right in the middle of my bunk. I kicked that guy as hard as I could right in the middle of his chest. Needless to say, I got roughed up pretty good but those four inmates knew they had been in a fight! I spent three days in the TU, but from that point on I didn't have any more trouble out of the gangs. When they find out that you will fight for yourself, they leave you alone. Unfortunately, there are too many others who won't fight.

The idea though of buying and selling inmates just got to me when I was in El Reno. I approached several other inmates on the issue and found that they felt the same way. We decided to do something about it. We knew that fighting the gangs for them was not the answer, so we determined another way. We began going to the gang leaders and asking to buy a certain individual. As soon as we purchased him, we would tell him to pay us back, a little at a time. In the meantime, he became his own person, and if anyone bothered him, we took care of it. The more inmates we bought, the more we had behind us. The more we had behind us, the easier it was to keep the gangs at bay. It wasn't long before men were approaching us and asking us to purchase them out of gang control.

When the administration learned of what we were doing, they called several of us in and asked us to serve on the inmate council. The council met with the new inmates in the A&O unit. We would go to them and let them know what to expect on the day that they moved into the general population. We told them just like it was, and we encouraged them to stand up for themselves and to break a few noses. In time, there were fewer and fewer new inmates winding up in the control of a gang. I am very proud to say now, after all these years, that is one thing that I will always be proud of doing. Even though I was in prison for breaking the law, I never had the desire to control another human's life. In the three years and five months that I was in El Reno, I helped set some 300 inmates free. Not to the outside world of course, but free from slavery and tyranny.

I earned two kinds of *good time* while at El Reno. *Statutory good time* was one, which is time off for good behavior. I also received *industrial good time*, given to any inmate that worked in Federal Prison Industries. With the *good time,* I had to serve only three years and five months of my five year term.

Nevada State Penitentiary

Upon my mandatory release, which means you served your time, less your good time, I went to live in Reno, Nevada. It didn't take me long to get into more criminal escapades. I got in with a fellow who was running hot goods from California to Utah. He told me about a fence (a person who buys stolen merchandise) in Oakland that he was working for. He said that if I drove a truck for the guy I could make a thousand dollars a load, and there was no loading or unloading of the truck involved.

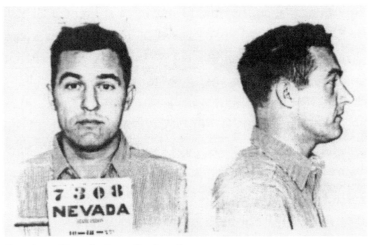

Darwin at Nevada State Penitentiary.

Well, I took him up on his offer. I was living with a showgirl in Nevada and we were very happy together. The money was great. I never knew what I was hauling and I didn't ask. The last load that I was scheduled to take to Utah turned out to be the best one. The fence had been picked up and was being held in a jail in California. I went to see him and he asked me if I would go to Oakland and pick up a house load of merchandise. It was evidence that could be used against him and I could have it all if I wanted it.

My plan was as follows: my girlfriend and I would take cars that had the back seats removed, to Oakland. We drove down, but once we got there and I saw all of the merchandise, we had to change our plans. There was no way all of that stuff would fit in two cars! I rented a truck and we filled it with the expensive goods. My girlfriend drove back to Reno and I went on to Provo, Utah, where I sold everything to another fence for five thousand dollars.

Shortly after that, my girl got an offer to work in Las Vegas, but she didn't want to go without me. My bankroll was fat after the Utah trip and so I told her if that's what you want, let's do it. When we got to Vegas, she went to work right away. Some of the girls that she was working with lived in a big house out in Henderson, Nevada. Some of them had men living there with them and they shared the rent. They asked my girlfriend if we would like to move in. We were staying in a motel and that wasn't cheap, so we decided to move in with them.

What a house that was! It was a continuous party day and night. The girls all worked different shifts, and some of them were always home. Someone was always cooking up a big meal or having food brought in. In time we became very good friends with one of the couples. The fellow was a casino manager at one of the small clubs on the outskirts of Las Vegas. He never seemed to have any money and I soon found out why.

One night he and his girlfriend had a huge misunderstanding, and I overheard her tell him that he had to stop gambling. When she stormed out to go to work, he mixed a drink and brought it to the room where we were. He suddenly began talking about robbing the club that he managed. He said that there was always about $10,000.00–

$15,000.00 in the safe at all times. That evening I strolled into his club to take a look around. It was small—there were only four blackjack tables and one craps table. Most of the business was at the bar. I had a few drinks and then I left to go pick up my girl downtown.

The next day the casino manager approached me at the house and asked me if I'd ever done any time. I said *yes*, and he said that he could tell by the way that I carried myself. Then he laid out his plan to rob his own club. He couldn't do it alone and he needed an accomplice. All I had to do was walk in the place and put all of the customers on the floor. He would have a bag of money ready to go. It seemed foolproof to me, so I agreed.

About midnight I walked into the club with a sawed-off shotgun. A silk stocking covered my face but I could see just fine. I put everyone on the floor and then I fired one shot into the ceiling. I yelled to the manager in the gruffest voice that I could muster to get me all of the money, now! True to his word, he had it ready, all sacked up in a canvas bank bag. I told the people on the floor to stay there and not to move, even if they heard the door close. I told them that the first one who did would "get it." I went out, got in my car, (I had covered up the license plates) and drove home. I sat down at the kitchen table and counted up the take. There was a little over $10,000.00 in the bag. When the casino manager came in at about 2:30 in the morning, we split the money and went to bed.

All the next day though I just couldn't shake the feeling that things weren't right. I tried going to several bars but the premonition just would not go away. I decided to hide my share of the money and so I stashed it in the trunk of my car. I picked up my girl from work and we stopped on the way home to get a bite to eat. We were pulling into the driveway of the big old house when cops came from everywhere. They arrested me, but let my girlfriend go. Maybe it doesn't sound like luck, but it was a lucky break for me. My money was in the car which they never searched. They booked me into the Clark County jail and when she came to visit me I told her to take it. She was a great gal and she stuck with me all the way down the line. I wanted her to have something for it.

At that time, Clark County didn't have much of a jail. It turned out that there were two guys in it that I had served time with in California. We promptly put our heads together and came up with a plan to escape. They kept all of the felony prisoners in a separate part of the jail together, and one day a week, there was only one jailer on duty. On that day, one of the guys made an appointment to meet with his lawyer. When the jailer came to get him, all of us grabbed the officer and got his keys. We locked him in the big cell.

We had made a plan to just walk over to the Fremont Hotel which was about two blocks away. We went in very casually and took the elevator to the fourth floor. We knocked gently on a door and when a man asked who it was, I replied, "Western Union." When he opened it, we all rushed inside. We told him to just keep quiet and do as we told him to and he wouldn't get hurt. We stayed in that room all night and all of the following day. That evening we tied the poor guy up, but I left a wake-up call at the desk for the following morning. I informed them that I was a very heavy sleeper and to be **sure** that they woke me as I had a very important business engagement that I just couldn't afford to miss.

When it was dark we went down to the street and hailed a couple of taxis. We planned to split up but to meet in front of the Sands Hotel on the Strip. Our cabbie was the talkative sort and he began telling us all about the breakout and that there were roadblocks on all of the roads leading out of Vegas. At the Sands, we reunited and over dinner we discussed our options. We briefly contemplated taking over another room but decided against it. Three of us liked the idea of walking out down the railroad tracks toward California and the other fellow chose to try his luck on his own.

We had walked the tracks for quite a distance when we came upon a little wooden shack with a dirty window. Inside we could just make out the form of a motorized handcar. We broke the lock and rolled the car out. Finding a ride put us all in a much better mood. We began singing *I've Been Working on the Railroad* and we were moving along at a pretty good rate of speed when I noticed that all of the signal lights along the track were red!

We stopped the handcar and looked at each other. We heard the train whistle. We tipped the hand car off the tracks and we followed it down the bank just as the wind from the train hit us from behind. I hate to think what would have happened if I hadn't suddenly noticed those signal lights!

The handcar was too heavy to lift back onto the tracks so we continued walking until daylight. When we spotted a grain elevator we crawled up underneath it and slept for several hours. The heat woke us up sometime around noon. Boy, was it hot! We didn't have any water or food and we were out of cigarettes. We just sat there for awhile trying to figure out our next move. We could see what looked like a filling station off in the distance. Since I had the cleanest clothes it was decided that I would walk over and get some sodas and candy bars. I walked down the tracks and as I got closer I could see that it was a service station and a grocery store. Past it, there was nothing but desert and it seemed like you could see for miles in any direction. The sign said *Jean, Nevada.* I knew then that we were about six miles from the California state line.

The only person inside the store was a little old man. I picked out some lunch meat, bread, apples and a half gallon of milk, along with several packs of cigarettes. When I left the store I walked in the opposite direction from where my buddies were hiding. Then I doubled back onto the tracks again. We had just finished eating when we heard a hound dog baying. In a few more seconds we saw a big old bloodhound coming right at us! Then we heard a bullhorn and saw a jeep! The dog came right under the building where we were. We fed him all of the lunch meat that we had left, hoping that he wouldn't attack us.

We crawled out from under the grain elevator with our hands up. Two of the officers in the jeep kept us covered with shotguns while the other one handcuffed us behind our backs. They marched us back to the store and made us wait in the sun until three Clark County squad cars pulled up. There wasn't much we could do with our hands cuffed behind us. The officers formed a circle with the three of us in the middle. They would pull us up and hit us until we fell down. I don't know how many times they hit us. The last thing I remember was someone kicking me and then I passed out.

By the time we reached Las Vegas, I was awake and spitting up blood. At the city jail where they took us this time, we were put into solitary cells. One of the jailers took pity on me and called a doctor. When the doctor arrived and saw how bad off I was he ordered them to take me to the hospital immediately. The other jailers refused, but the doctor got angry and threatened to have their badges. At that, they complied.

The doctors and nurses at the hospital were appalled to see that the police would beat someone so badly. They said that they would testify on my behalf if I wanted to file charges. There wasn't much that they could do for me except to take x-rays and give me pain medication. I was black and blue from my shoulders clear down to my knees. I had cuts all over my face, especially around my eyes. They had to put stitches in both of my eyebrows. They kept me there for three days and took pictures of all my injuries. I had every intention of filing charges against the Clark County Sheriff's Department.

After a day or two in solitary confinement, some officers came in and told me that if I would plead guilty to the original armed robbery charge, the judge would give me a sentence of from five to six years. I agreed, and the next morning I went before the judge who sentenced me to five years and not more than six. The very next day, I was in the state penitentiary at Carson City, Nevada. There they put me in lock-up and kept me isolated. Every few days the captain would come in and asked me if I was still going to file charges. Every day I said that I was. Finally, he told me that unless I changed my mind I would serve out my sentence in lock-up, in solitary confinement.

My two buddies began sending me notes by the inmate who brought my food. They said that they were already planning their next escape and they wanted me to get out of lock-up so that I could go with them. I had been there about three months, so I told the cell-house guard to let me see the captain. I got out of there the same day when I told him what he wanted to hear.

The Nevada state prison system was run by con

bosses. The warden assigned inmates to run the departments within the prison. The inmates hired their own crews. Jobs were a privilege because there weren't that many to be had. One of my buddies, Al, had bought himself a job in the kitchen and he was living in a dormitory on the top floor of the cell house. He and another guy were digging a tunnel in one of the back walls. It was protected from sight by a row of sinks that ran across the back wall of the mess hall. They weren't having much success though because there was so little time available to work on it.

Getting things in prison was really easy if you had the money to pay for them. You could get anything you wanted, even a woman. The women inmates were housed on the third floor of the hospital building. For fifty dollars the night sergeant would check you into the hospital and open the steel door that led to the women's quarters. Sometimes you got lucky and a young, pretty woman would be *on-call.* Other nights you might not be so lucky!

I too bought myself a kitchen job so that I could help with the tunnel but work on it was moving really slowly. One day, I just happened to be sick and lying in bed in the dormitory when by accident I saw the way out of the prison. It was the rule for the inmates, at meal times, to file into the mess hall. The captain would stand at the door and check you off as you called out your number. This was called *the count board.* Everyone had their place in the line and you had to be in it. If you were sick, you were checked off on the count board ahead of time. There were two gun cages, one on each end of the mess hall, each with a guard carrying a shotgun. When all of the inmates were counted off, they locked the barred door, so that for the duration of the meal, which was for an hour, all of the inmates were locked in. While I was watching, the doors were locked and then the guards manning the guard towers left their posts. After a full hour, the guards came back and the mess hall doors were unlocked. A lightbulb went off in my head. I had the way out! There was a whole hour during meals when no one was watching the outer walls.

I told Al the new plan and we set about to get some hacksaw blades. My girl was coming up from Vegas to see me and she was very generous with the money that I had given her. I bribed a minimum security inmate who worked downtown in the Governor's Mansion and he just walked down to the hardware store in Carson City and bought some! The very next day, my friend and I both faked illnesses, and sawed away at one of the bars on our cell window. We never cut it completely, but just enough so that it would take only a minute to complete the cut. After that, we spent a few days buying up all of the *green money* in the prison that we could. *Green money* is regular money and there was a lot of it on the inside. We needed as much regular money as we could get so that we could get out of the area once we made our escape.

Finally the day came and we both claimed to be sick. We sawed the rest of the bar on the window, watched as the guards left their towers, and then we were on our way. Using the other barred windows as steps, we went down the side of the building, climbed over the back wall and finally over a fence. There was nothing now in front of us but desert. We just started running. Finally we came to an irrigation ditch, and as it was so hot, we dove right in. Boy, did that water feel good! On the other side of the ditch was a hay field. We saw a grove of trees and headed that way. The trees were grouped around a farm and a ranch house.

When we got to the house, we saw a note on the door saying that they would be back the next day. Lady Luck was smiling on us! The door was open and we went in. We found clothes and a shotgun, and the keys to a Ford station wagon in the garage. We raided the refrigerator where we found a beef roast and a carton of milk. We then headed towards Reno where we knew we could trade the car for another one. I knew a doorman there who could get us a car that wouldn't be missed for a few days.

I drove right up to the hotel where he was standing out front and when he opened the car door, he almost fainted. "I thought you two guys were in the joint," he said. "Well, we were until about three hours ago!" I replied. We told him what we needed and he took some keys off of a peg board and said to wait, he'd be right back. He soon pulled up in a new car and got out. He said, "Good luck to the both of you," and we drove away, headed for California and the Oregon border.

On the way we broke into some businesses but didn't get much in the way of money. We did however, get a .45-caliber handgun with an extra clip at a car dealership. When we got to Oregon, we bought some tools at a hardware store in a small town and spent the day sleeping in a park under some shade trees. When it got dark, we hit several businesses looking for cash, but couldn't find anything substantial. We had worked up quite an appetite so we went into a Chinese restaurant for dinner. We had just gotten back to the car when we noticed all of the lights in the restaurant go out. We had been the last customers. "Maybe we should check that place out," I said.

Finally, two people came out and drove away. We went to the back of the building and jimmied the door. We went into the office and as it turned out, everything we touched was loaded with money! There was a bookcase in the office and if we picked up a book and shook it, money fell out. There was so much money that we had to get a tablecloth to put it all in. Up the road at a motel, we stopped to count it. There was over ten thousand dollars! Now we had some traveling money. We kept hearing news broadcasts on the radio about the two convicts who had escaped from Carson City. We knew if we could make it to Portland we could catch a train that went to Chicago. We had been locked up a long time though and we had ten thousand dollars. We decided that we deserved a party before we got on that train.

In Portland, we pulled into a parking lot across from a nice looking hotel. We had been putting all of the coins from the businesses that we broke into, into a canvas bag. It was so heavy that I warned my partner not to set it down in the hotel for fear a bell hop might pick it up and get suspicious. While we were crossing the street to go to the hotel, the bottom of the bag fell out! My buddy stopped to try and pick it up but I grabbed his arm and we just kept on going! We went in the front door of the hotel and right out the back! I hailed a cab and we went right to the train station. I didn't breathe a sigh of relief until the train pulled out and we were squirreled away in sleeping compartments.

Once we arrived in Chicago, we found a nice little hotel that we liked so much, we decided that if we ever got split up, we'd meet there when we could. In the bar, we met a couple of gals who were staying at the hotel too. We all had a good time for the next couple of days. They told us that they were *schoolteachers* and we told them that we were *businessmen*.

We weren't hurting for money so later on we went over to a dealership and paid cash for a brand new 1957 automobile. It came with all the extras and cost us $4800.00. We left the hotel then and headed towards Iowa, my old stomping grounds. The new car had cut pretty heavily into our bankroll, so we were thinking about our next move. In Illinois we stopped in a small town to get something to eat. We went into a coffee shop right on the main street. We were sitting there eating when we realized that right across from us was a bank. We just kept eating and looking and then Al said to me, "Are you thinking what I'm thinking?"

Out at the car I said, "Well what do you think Al? Should we rob that bank?" In his matter-of-fact way, Al said, "I don't see why not." We got the guns out of the suitcase in the trunk of the car and pulled up to the front of the bank. When we walked in, all we could see were two people, a young woman and an older man. The young woman walked over and I told her that I was there to see the bank president on business. When the older man came out of his small glassed-in office, he was all smiles until I pulled the gun from my pocket.

I told him to open the vault and to make it quick. He opened it right up and I stood there dumb-faced. I didn't have anything to put the money into! I grabbed a waste paper basket and emptied the contents on the floor. I ordered the bank president to fill it up and he did just that. Meanwhile, Al got the money out of the drawers where the teller worked. We then put the woman in the vault with the president and locked them both inside . I found a piece of cloth under the counter and I threw that over the money in the waste basket. We walked calmly to the car, got in and drove away. We kept moving all night long.

When the sun came up, we saw a sign for Omaha. We drove into downtown where we found the Hill Hotel. We wanted a place to stay and get some rest. In the parking lot we emptied the money out of the trash can into a suitcase and put the guns in with it. We then went in and got adjoining rooms. I was beat from driving all night, so I took a shower and went to bed. A short time later I was awakened by Al who had two women with him. He had gone down to the bar and apparently found some more schoolteachers.

When I had time later on to count the money, I was amazed to see that we had over $46,000.00! I immediately went on a shopping spree and bought us a bunch of new clothes. Al and I were the same size so I knew what to get. Then we partied with those new schoolteacher gals for several days. They really liked the way we threw our money around. One night we were in a bar drinking when one of the gals asked when we were leaving Omaha. I fed her a big story about going to Florida for a couple of weeks. Well, then she asked if they could go with us. Before I could answer, *"No,"* Al piped up and said that they could! You see he was not only sweet on his schoolteacher gal, he was in love!

We took off the next day not really caring where we were going. We just drove until we found someplace that we liked and we would stay a few days and then move on. I think it took us about two weeks before we finally got to Florida. We stopped in Jacksonville and that was as far as we got before we turned and headed back towards Chicago. The hotel employees where we had stayed before were glad to see us as they knew we were big tippers. We winded up staying about ten days there before we left for Omaha. Al was madly in love and he bought that girl of his so much stuff that I was beginning to wonder how we would get it all in the car!

In Omaha we checked back into the Hill Hotel and the gals said that they had to check on their apartment and pay the rent. We gave them the money and told them to call us when they had all of their business squared away. I went to bed and slept peacefully all night. I woke up pretty early and went down alone to the coffee shop for breakfast. Afterwards, as I was standing by the counter in the lobby to get cigarettes, I noticed two guys in business suits talking to the desk clerk. One of the men pulled a couple of photos out of a briefcase. Lo and behold, those photos were of me and Al!

I took off out of there and went into the lobby of a different hotel. I quickly dialed Al's room number. It took him some time to answer. I was beginning to worry that I was already too late to warn him when he picked up the receiver. I told him to get out right now because the FBI was at the front desk asking about us!

I jumped in a taxi and went across the bridge into Council Bluffs, Iowa. Then I got on a Greyhound bus leaving for Chicago. Our car was still parked in the parking lot of the hotel with our guns and money in the trunk. I was sure hoping that Al would get the car, but I found out later that he didn't. I checked back into the little hotel where we had stayed before and promised to meet each other if we got split up. I figured that in a couple of days he would appear.

In those days you could buy *anything* on Maxwell Street in Chicago, so I went down and bought a couple of guns. Every day I'd sit in the bar where I could watch the street and the entrance to the hotel. A week went by. Every day I bought the Omaha paper to see if they had arrested Al. Eight days passed. Then nine. On the tenth day, I was perched on my usual corner bar stool watching the front door when a yellow cab pulled out, and guess who got out? I was never so happy to see someone in my entire life!

Later he told me that he had given that gal of his all of the money that he had on him, figuring to get more out of the car later. When I called, he had grabbed his clothes and run down the stairs. When he got out of the hotel he had run down the street toward the railroad tracks and then jumped into an open boxcar of a train that was passing through town. He had finally wound up somewhere down in Kentucky and had to break into quite a few places to get enough money to get back to Chicago.

We took stock of what we had and it amounted to about four hundred dollars. We had the guns that I bought down on Maxwell Street, but we really needed a car. There was a fellow who was always hanging around the bar in the hotel. I asked him if he had a car and when he said that he did, I asked him if he would rent it to me so that I could take my friend home. At first he refused but we kept buying him drinks and finally he agreed to lend it to us for fifty dollars.

The next morning Al and I set out in the borrowed car looking for a bank to rob. This time I prepared ahead of time and took along a bag for the cash. We drove about eighty miles outside of Chicago and settled on another bank in another little town. We entered and walked up to the counter. This time there were three people in the bank. A woman approached and again I asked to speak to the bank president. We repeated the same scenario as before, locked the employees in the vault and then high-tailed it back to the Windy City. Back at the hotel, when we counted the take, we didn't have as much as the last time, but it wasn't bad. We got $22,000.00 and change. I gave the guy who owned the car his keys back and he was never the wiser!

The next day we went out and bought another new car and then we went shopping for new clothes . We had left everything behind when we had to bail out of Omaha ahead of the FBI. Al really wanted to go to Omaha to see that gal, but we decided that that was a little too dangerous, so we went to Kansas City, Missouri instead, and there we rented an apartment. We thought that might turn out to be safer than staying in hotels all of the time. In Kansas City, we frequented bars and met some more women. Al, it seemed, kept falling in love with every one he met.

One of them was very pretty and she had moved in with him. They seemed to be getting along fine, but she soon put the two of us on the outs again. One night she slipped away from him on the pretense that she had to go and see her mother. A couple of days passed and she still hadn't come back. I was getting short on pocket money so I went to the closet where we kept the suitcase that held the money and the guns. There was no suitcase! She had obviously taken it with her.

We were short again, but since I had lived in Sioux City as a kid, I was pretty sure that we could get some guns on credit from a guy that I knew there. When I called him he said, "Sure, come on over!" We drove out to his place and there he had several sawed-off shotguns and plenty of handguns. We took one shotgun and two of the handguns. I promised him that I'd be back with the money, but that I couldn't stick around too long as the law in those parts knew me and I was pretty sure that they were on the look-out for me.

Back in Kansas City we stopped for breakfast, and wouldn't you know it, right across from the restaurant was a bank! It was early in the morning so the bank wasn't yet open, so we just sipped coffee and waited. When a couple of employees opened up, we paid for breakfast and then casually sauntered over, and then we entered on the coattails of a woman customer as if we were with her. The employees were just opening up, so they were walking around with open trays full of money. We ordered them all down as before and I filled another waste basket with green paper. Then we locked them all in the vault, walked nonchalantly back to the car and drove away. It was like taking candy from babies.

I told Al that we should go to Sioux City and pay the guy for the guns. We got a motel room there, and when I paid the guy, he asked me how much money I got from the bank. I looked at him and said, "What bank?" We both got a good laugh out of that. Back at the hotel again, Al and I counted up $34,000.00. The downside was that Iowa, Nebraska and Ilinois were getting pretty hot for us, so we decided to go south. I suggested Texas, but Al's folks lived there and he didn't want to go. Then he remembered that his parents had a log cabin in Arkansas. He phoned to ask them about it, and his mother said that the police had been over to their place several times looking for him. She gave him directions to the cabin and we set out to find it. Al's Dad was an ex-con so we knew that they wouldn't turn us in.

It took us a couple of days but we made it there. The property was backed by the Ozark National Forest. To me the area seemed like hillbilly country. I had never seen folks like the ones who lived around there except in the movies. We took a bunch of supplies up to the cabin, but we took trips into town to buy lumber as we were going to fix the place up. It was a log cabin made from trees that had grown right on the property and because no one had lived in it for awhile it needed a little patching in places.

It was February and the nights got really cold. All we had were sleeping bags and it took us a few days to nail enough siding on to hold in the heat. One morning I was awakened by something wet hitting me in the face. It was still too dark out to see what it was so I rolled over and went back to sleep. When I woke up later, I had a pile of snow on top of me from where it had fallen in through the holes in the roof! Needless to say, I went up and repaired them the same day.

We had a couple of chain saws, so we cut a lot of firewood. We didn't have to walk far to get it. One day, I was up on the roof again, doing some more repairs, when a whole pack of hound dogs came bounding into the yard and ran right into the cabin. I heard someone give a holler and when I looked down I saw an old gentleman standing in the yard. Al came up from the creek where he was cutting wood and I came down off the roof to see what he wanted. The old man looked us over and said as how he reckoned we was the boys who bought the place. He was carrying a brown jug and from time to time he tipped it up as we were talking. Finally he offered us a swig.

"What's in it?" I asked.

"Why corn whisky, sonny," he said.

I took the jug and took a long drink. Boy, was it smooth!

"I make it my own self," he said, and then he asked if we had any beer about.

I went down to the creek where we kept a burlap bag full of beer cooling in the creek water and brought it back to the house. After a bit more whiskey and a few more beers, he finally got around to asking about what he had come for. He had heard the whine of the chain saws and wanted to know if we would be willing to trade one for some of his corn whiskey. Would we! We followed him back to his place up the creek aways, where we met his sister and sampled some more of the corn. The sister hit me up for a pouch of tobacco that I had on me and we got a kick out of watching her roll homemade cigarettes. She had a jug which she tipped frequently too, and a warm smile, even though all of her teeth were missing. We carried a full keg of the corn whiskey home with us along with the feeling that we had made a couple of friends for life.

Well word must have got out about us for just a few days later an old car came splashing through the creek and almost ran right into the cabin before it stopped. There were five men in the car and just by looking at them I could tell that they had to be brothers. They all looked just alike. They told us that they had just come back from town where they had sold some of the animal furs that they got from trapping. They were all pretty drunk. Wanting to be neighborly, we offered them some beer and some of our corn whiskey. I figured that it was what they had come for anyway. As it turned out they had a sister about twenty years old and when she came around, Al promptly fell in love again. After awhile she was at our place more than she was at home.

When the weather got nice, we started going into town at night. It was a college town full of young people looking for a good time. Everyone seemed curious about Al and me. We told them that we were just up there working on his folks' cabin. Pretty soon we had as many as four or five carloads of kids showing up on the weekends looking for a party. During one of these occasions when there must have been about a dozen of us drinking and carrying on, the Moore brothers' big old car rolled into the yard and the five brothers all leaped out and held onto it to get it to stop. They could barely stand up, they were all so drunk, and they were excited.

In the trunk of their car, they had a big boar possum, the biggest one that I had ever seen. They said for all of us to come on and go up the creek with them, which we all did. We tried to be quiet but there was so much splashing and giggling that it was impossible. Finally we got to the old man's place that had traded us the whiskey for the chain saw. We could see him through an open window snoring, with those hound dogs lying all over him. In fact, the house was so old and decrepit that there were more open spaces than not.

We all hid in the trees and bushes and did our best not to make any noise. One of the brothers snuck up to the house and gently tossed the possum onto the bed right in the middle of all those hounds. Well, you never heard such a commotion in all of your life! The hounds were baying, the old man was hollering, and then suddenly a shotgun went off in the house and shingles on the roof went flying! Well, we did our best to skedaddle out of there, but we were all laughing so hard that we fell over each other in the creek trying to get away. The old man came over to our place the next day. Fortunately he was over his mad spell and he was even able to laugh at himself. He swore he'd get even with those Moore boys though.

Al and I enjoyed going into town to party too, and a lot of times we'd have some of the corn whiskey in the evening and then decide that we wanted to go to town. We tried to be careful about drinking and driving as we knew that it wasn't the smartest thing to do. One day I hit on a solution. While I was sober, I climbed up into a big tree in the front yard, hammered a nail into the trunk and then hung the car keys on the nail. I reasoned that if we were too drunk to climb up and get the keys, we were too drunk to drive. A few days later, sure enough, we were drinking and Al said he wanted to go into town. I told him to crawl up and get the keys. He tried, but he would get only a few feet up before he slid right back down. Finally, he looked at me funny, said, "Wait just a minute," and he disappeared into the house. When he came out, he had a rifle, but as he never was much of a shot, I didn't think anything about it. Well, he took aim and fired. Those keys flew every which way! It took us three days to find all of them. But my theory worked: we didn't go to town that night!

Then one day the county sheriff drove out just checking on things. I told Al that it was time we moved on. We really hated to leave. We gave the Moore brothers and the old man and his sister just about everything that we had, and they couldn't thank us enough. We set out for the West Coast, but when we got to Salt Lake City, the weather was so nice that we stayed there for awhile. Then we went on into Nevada where we intended to do a little gambling. We didn't dare go anywhere near Reno or Carson City, so we ended up at Elko instead. That turned out to be a real mistake.

Al started gambling and giving all of our money away to women that he fell in love with. Pretty soon we were almost completely broke. We never did fight over money though: when the suitcase got low we just filled it up again! So we headed back towards Chicago, since things always seemed to go better for us there. We kept our eyes open for a bank to rob along the way. When we found a likely candidate, we took some time and actually planned the stick-up.

We got a clipboard and some lined paper and laid out an escape route where we never had to cross a major highway. We even drove around and wrote down the number of speedometer miles and which way to turn. We felt pretty sure of ourselves. The day of the robbery we parked down the street and waited for the bank to open. Then we went inside and it was business as usual. We got away following our map to the letter. By noon we were a hundred miles down the road so we pulled over and counted the take. Al had guessed that we had $25,000.00 and I guessed $30,000.00, so we were a little disappointed to find only $18,000.00 in the bag. In Chicago we rented two apartments and bought another car so that we would both have one.

There was a nice looking gal living in the complex. I had noticed her several times and I wanted to meet her, but it seemed like an opportunity never presented itself. One night I was in a bar in the neighborhood when she came in and to my surprise , came over and sat down on the stool next to me. She let me buy her a drink and I told her that I had seen her around and was hoping to meet her. She said that she had seen me around too, and wanted to get to know me. We went to a little Italian café, had dinner, and one thing led to another.

A week later we were living together. When Al found out I was living with a girl, he said, "Well, it's about time!" He had another new one every week it seemed and was in fact living in a hotel with a new one when I caught up with him. The four of us started to spend a lot of time together and we even went down to Mexico for awhile. We were spending a lot of money though, so Al and I started planning our next bank job. We left the girls some money and told them that we had to take care of some cattle business in Montana.

Though he was probably never aware of the part that he played, a marshal in the small town of the aptly named *Correctionville,* put an end to my criminal career. In fact, this last bank job that my partner and I pulled there, almost put an end to us. Later, my case made legal history and I came within a hair of getting the death penalty for it.

Ironically, earlier that day we had driven up and down the practically empty streets of the village searching for the marshal. Our plan was to pick him up and force him to accompany us out into the country to the bank president's house. We drove for over an hour looking for him in vain. We couldn't have gotten arrested if we tried. We had cased the place thoroughly. Through a gun dealer friend of ours in Sioux City we learned that the bank had an alarm system that hadn't worked in years. The same was true of the booster safe in the vault. The dealer also said that the town had only one marshal on duty at night and that he didn't even wear a gun. Furthermore, the bank president handled all of the rental property in the town. If we went to the bank and told him that we were looking for some offices to rent, then that would give us an excuse to go to his house at some point, take him hostage, and then make him accompany us to the bank later, after hours. It all sounded too good to be true. It was a Friday so the gun guy, whose name was Shorty Hart, suggested that we stay the weekend with him. Al went out and found some women who came back with him and we spent the weekend carousing. Finally, on Sunday night, we took them home and tried to get a good night's rest. I was worried about Al who had been drinking a lot but I pushed any trepidation that I had, away, and tried to sleep.

About noon the next day, we went boldly into the bank and introduced ourselves as businessmen looking for offices to rent. The bank president was more than happy to take us around town, showing us what he had to offer. Finally we said that we would have to talk it over with our wives before we made a final decision and asked if it was okay to get back to him that evening. He responded that that was no problem and promptly wrote down the directions to his house for us which was out in the country. After that, we drove to another small town about fifteen miles away and passed the remainder of the day playing pool. When it got dark out, we drove back to Correctionville and after spending the futile hour searching for the marshal we gave up and following the directions that he had so generously provided for us, we went directly to the bank president's house.

His wife opened the door smiling, but the smile quickly vanished as we pulled our guns out. I told them to co-operate and they wouldn't get hurt. Then I demanded that the bank president write down the combinations to the door of the vault and to the safe inside.

The poor man was shaking so badly that he could hardly comply with my orders. Then I had him produce the keys to the bank. He handed me a large ring and indicated which key opened the front door. Then I gave it to Al and sent him into town to get the money.

The three of us sat in the farmhouse kitchen and smoked nervously while we waited. About half an hour passed and then Al came bursting through the front door mad as an old wet hen! He started yelling that the president had given us the wrong combination to the safe! The banker pleaded with us not to harm them, and insisted that it *was* the right combination, but the safe was old and that it was very difficult to get it to open. I decided then to go myself and to take the banker with me. If I had stopped to consider that this spontaneous decision would qualify as kidnaping and carry a possible death penalty, maybe I would have sent Al back again by himself. At any rate, Al stayed with the wife and when we arrived at the bank, the president did everything that I told him to. It took him several tries to open the safe so I knew that he had been telling the truth. Back safely at his house, I asked him how much cash was in the safe and he said that there was fifty thousand dollars. I sent Al back to load the money. When he returned we placed the couple on the bed and taped their hands and feet. I took a couple of wash cloths from the bathroom, folded them in half and taped them over their mouths. Then we jumped in the car and headed for Sioux City. We thought that we had gotten away scot free, but now our failure to locate that small town marshal was going to come back to haunt us.

As it turned out, while Al was inside the bank, the marshal happened to drive by, noticing the strange car parked outside. Not recognizing it as one of the local's, he wrote down the license plate number and called it in to the Iowa Highway Patrol. A little while later on his rounds, he noticed that the car was gone, so he called again to see if they had stopped it. They hadn't, so they then asked the Sioux City Police to be on the lookout for it. By the time we pulled into Sioux City off highway 20, several patrol cars were waiting for us. One of the units flashed its spotlight across our windshield and activated its siren.

I yelled, "Hang on, Al, we're going for a ride!" and floored the accelerator.

The patrol car came up fast in the rearview mirror and I shouted for Al to do something! He responded by rolling down his window and firing off some rounds from his .45 automatic. This caused the cops to drop back almost a full block behind us. We both started to stuff money into our shirts in preparation for bailing out of the vehicle. As we came up fast on my old neighborhood, I warned Al to be ready. Then I executed a quick left turn and hit the brakes. Our car slid into the curb, jumped straight up into the air, came down hard onto some grass and stopped dead. Two more patrol cruisers flew up. Al stepped out and found himself looking down the barrel of a shotgun. I took off running down the street.

I could hear footsteps behind me and then I felt bullets whizzing past my ears. Then we both stopped and I realized that he probably had an empty gun. I stopped right in the middle of the street and turned and fired into the air. He turned and ran and then so did I. I didn't stop again until I reached the entrance to the storm sewers that I had explored as a kid while playing hooky instead of going to school. I was safe.

Down in the sewers, I knew that I would soon reach the river for that is where they emptied out. I rearranged the money in my shirt and put the two guns in my front pockets of my pants. I knew that I didn't dare show my face around town for now that they had Al, they'd know that they were looking for me. I decided to take the railroad tracks leading to Omaha. I figured that if I could walk fifteen or twenty miles then I could look for another car. I walked all night and when the sun came up, I hid in a cornfield and went to sleep. I stayed there all day and when it got dark, I started walking again. The tracks ran parallel to a highway and pretty soon I saw a cafe´ up ahead. I needed to eat something and I could use some cigarettes so I decided to give it a try. I was sure that I had walked over ten miles so it would probably be safe. There was only one pickup truck parked out front, so I went in.

There was one old man and a woman inside. She told

me that the cook wasn't in yet but she'd fix me something. I ordered what the old guy was having as it looked pretty good. Then while I was eating, they were talking and I heard him say that he was going to Omaha to get some tractor parts. I asked him for a ride and he said *sure*. We had only gone about fifteen miles however, when we ran into a roadblock. After they checked the driver's ID they turned their attention to me. When I stepped out of the car several of the cops leaned over their hoods and pointed shotguns at me.

I had a phoney ID which I handed over. Then one of them asked me what I had in my front pockets. I said, "Shaving gear." They bent me over the car hood and frisked me, finding the two guns and the money. They asked me where I got the money and I said, "You're the smart guys, you figure it out!" I got a punch in the ribs for that, hand-cuffs and leg irons and then they threw me into the squad car. Down at the station, I wouldn't talk though and I didn't admit anything. Just when I began to worry that they were going to resort to force, two federal marshals came and took custody of me. They booked me into the Woodbury County Jail.

Al was in there already, in a tank in the back, but on the same floor. He'd had pretty much the same experience that I had but he said that he didn't tell them anything. He warned me that there was an intercom system and that it was better to pass notes through a trustee who did the cleaning, than to talk. I went to sleep and slept for a day and a half. A guard finally shook me awake and we were both taken in leg irons and cuffs before the federal commissioner who read off the charges against us. Back in a holding cell, Al whispered to me that some of the guys in the tank were going to grab the jailer and make a break for it.

The next morning they grabbed him and got the keys. They had forgotten about the intercom though and he started yelling his head off. We took an elevator to the basement but found the metal door down there locked. It would have taken too long to try every key on the ring, so we tried bending a corner of the metal sheet. We got a hole just big enough to squeeze through but there was still one more door leading to the street. From the landing we could see an officer waiting for us with a shotgun aimed and ready. We fled back down the stairs and I ran into a supply room that had a lot of cabinets on the walls. I opened one of the cabinets and crawled in. I piled the contents in front of me and kept still.

Throughout the day I heard them searching for me and one time someone even opened the cabinet door and looked in! I didn't dare move a muscle. Another time, two of them stood in front of the cabinet and smoked a cigarette and I heard from their conversation that they had caught the other guys. Al apparently told them that I had run off down the street, but they weren't buying it because of that officer with the gun.

Finally I dozed off, and then I heard them come back

into the room. This time they were really searching. All of a sudden they opened my cabinet door, moved aside the books and things and saw my face. I don't know which of us was the more surprised. They pulled their weapons, cuffed me and took me up to the main floor. The place was swarming with armed policemen. I learned later that they were all over the roof and everything. It was a good thing that I had sat tight! They put Al and me back upstairs in the tank, but this time they posted a guard armed with a shotgun.

We sat there for three days and then a federal lawyer came to talk to us. He said that if we would agree to plead guilty to the bank robbery, we would get fifteen years. He also explained to us that by forcing the bank president to go with me to the bank, we had committed a capital offense and could get the death penalty if we went to trial! I asked Al what he thought. He said he thought fifteen years sounded good to him. We told the lawyer to tell the DA that he had a deal. An hour later federal marshals arrived to take us to the courthouse. They gave us each a pair of white coveralls. On the front and on the back were the words **FEDERAL PRISONER** in bold lettering. We were again handcuffed and put in leg irons.

They walked us across the street to the federal courthouse. The local television stations were there with the cameras rolling, all wanting a glimpse of the two desperados for the evening news. Inside the judge asked us how we pleaded and we said, "Guilty." Then he asked us if anyone had made us any promises or deals as to what our sentences would be. At this the lawyer leaned over to us and said, "You have to say *no*." Well, we did and then the judge sentenced us both to twenty years!

We both exclaimed, "Wait a minute!"

But the judge said, "Didn't you just tell me that no one had made you any promises?"

I said, "Yes, that is what we said, but . . ."

"Then let the record show that no promises were made!" he said, and then he went on to sentence us on several counts, including attempted escape and assault on a federal officer. Then he told the marshals to take us away.

5

Federal Penitentiary, Leavenworth, Kansas

The next morning bright and early, we were back in the white coveralls, handcuffs and leg irons, on our way to the federal penitentiary at Leavenworth in the state of Kansas. We stopped to eat in some small town in Nebraska. The marshals said that we could order anything that we wanted, and knowing that it would be awhile before I could sink my teeth into a juicy steak again, that's what I ordered. Al got one too. The handcuffs were attached to belts around our waists, making it very difficult for us to eat. Seeing this, two of the wait-

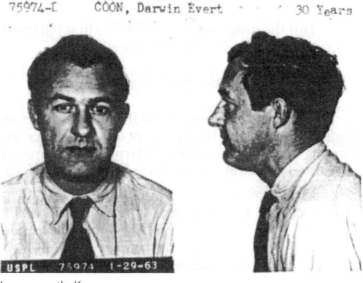

75974-I   COON, Darwin Evert   30 Years

USPL   75974 1-29-63

Leavenworth, Kansas.

resses came over and one helped Al and the other one helped me. The marshals didn't say anything but we could tell that they didn't like it. We thanked them afterwards and Al may even have fallen in love again!

"I have a brother in prison," one of the girls told us. "I hope that if he's ever in the same situation that someone will be kind enough to feed him."

We got to Leavenworth that afternoon. Going up the big front steps, Al fell and skinned both of his knees. It was almost impossible to walk up those steps while wearing leg irons. Once we were in the associate warden's office, he made it clear to us that the first wrong step we made, we'd be on our way to that little island out in the middle of San Francisco Bay. He warned us not to try to cell together or even to work in the same facility.

We did our admission orientation time in lock-up in C cell house. First we were strip searched, tossed some clothes and given our numbers. I was number 75974. Then they took us to C cell house which was a single cell housing unit. We found out later that that was where they kept most of the *girl/boys*. We spent thirty-two days in C block. I went to work in the laundry and Al went to work in the kitchen. Later I was moved to B cell house. Al stayed in C and the only time we could see each other was in the yard. We did see each other at mealtimes too, but just long enough to say hi.

We both had money on the books when we escaped from Nevada, so we wrote asking the authorities to send it to us. They did, and so at least now we had money for cigarettes. After only five months though, Al got into a fight in the kitchen, and true to the warden's word, they shipped him off to Alcatraz. I didn't care much for working in the laundry. I knew an inmate who worked in the plumbing shop, so I put in for a job change to there. The boss of the plumbing shop turned out to be a really nice guy and I enjoyed working for him. We had our coffee all the time, which was a real luxury, and when we had the chance to steal meat out of the kitchen, we would have a good old-fashioned cookout. The boss would even eat with us, no questions asked. If there was no work to do, we could go to the yard. If he needed us, all he had to do was to come to the yard and find one of us and he'd round up the rest of the crew.

One day, I was sitting in the yard, minding my own business, when I saw the *goon squad* coming. They dragged me to the hole and I didn't have the slightest idea why. The hole was not much fun to be in. It had a one-piece combination sink and stool and that was it. You were handed a pair of coveralls that could be any size, and which usually turned out to be either too big or too small for you. At seven in the evening the door opened and you went to the mattress pile and picked one. At seven the next morning, you took it back. The food was terrible but you had no choice. If you didn't eat it, you'd better flush it down the stool. They fed you like they were slopping hogs—they just piled everything into a loaf pan and it was always cold. We were fed twice a day but it wasn't something that we looked forward to.

The second night that I was in there, about midnight, my door opened and in came four big officers, all wearing baseball catcher's gear. They had on face masks, chest protectors and shin guards. I guessed that meant that I was the ball. They told me that I had a date to talk to the warden in the morning but first they were going to loosen my tongue a little. Then they proceeded to work me over. There was nothing I could do but take it. Finally they left. I could hear them laughing as they removed their gear.

The next morning the warden asked me what had happened to the tools that were missing from the plumbing shop. I didn't even know what he was talking about and told him so. He ordered me back to the hole and a few nights later the goon squad came back and worked me over again. Of course I still couldn't give them the information that they wanted, and this was repeated over the course of twenty-nine more days. That was the maximum time that they could keep you in the hole. They could take you out for one day though, and then put you right back in again. On the twenty-ninth day, the warden informed me that he was transferring me. He didn't say where, but I knew it had to be to **the Rock.**

I was sent upstairs in the prison and it was much better than the hole. You could buy candy and cigarettes from the commissary, and though it was nothing to brag about, the food was better. At least it was hot, and you got fed three times a day. You had a bunk to sleep in and a sink with a stool. No one came in the night and used me for a punching bag. After fifteen days I was taken to the showers and told to prepare for my transfer. There was a black guy in there with me and he said, "You know where we're going!" He had spent nine years out on the Rock, been released, got into trouble and now he was headed back for two more. As it turned out, he was the black Mafia leader from New York City. He had been sent back to prison for income tax violations.

They chained the two of us to three other inmates and put us on a prison bus to Wichita, Kansas. At Wichita, we boarded a train, along with our escort of four heavily armed guards. We were on the train for three nights and two days. They had to take the leg irons off so that we could climb up into the bunks to go to sleep but we were handcuffed at all times. Every one of us had swollen wrists and ankles. We got off the train in Richmond, California. They took us down to the waterfront in a police van. The prison boat, the *Warden Johnson,* was waiting for us. It was just a short ride across the bay to Alcatraz.

Next, we got on an old school bus that took us on a steep ride up to the top of the island. Five or six officers were standing in front of the prison. Without ceremony, they ushered us through a solid steel door with an electric lock. Then we had to wait for a key to be lowered down so that an officer could open a barred gate in front of us. We went into a room where they removed the handcuffs and leg irons. I was so happy to get those things off that I didn't care where I was. Then we were strip- searched and marched naked to the showers. After that, we were taken to *fish row* where we were each assigned to a cell in an area that came to be known to us as *Broadway*. When the steel door clanged shut behind me, the cold reality of where I was hit me. I was on **the Rock.** I was twenty-six years old.

Alcatraz

Each of us was given a rule book and told to read it. We had *standing count* three times a day. When the count bell rang, the inmate had to stand up to the bars of his cell with both hands pushed through the bars. He stood there until he heard the *all clear* bell ring. The first time that an inmate missed a standing count, he got a warning. The second time, he got three days in the *TU*, the Treatment Unit. There were three counts each day, one at 7:30 a.m., one at 11:45 a.m. and one at 3:30 p.m. In addition, we were all fingerprinted and given our numbers. My number was and is **AZ 1422**.

A pleasant surprise at Alcatraz was how good the

The End of the Line, Alcatraz.

food was. That first day I searched through the sea of faces in the mess hall for my buddy, Al, but I couldn't find him. I did see several other guys that I knew though. Back on Broadway, I was resting on my bunk reading the rule book when all of a sudden a bunch of books and clothes and other things came flying down right in front of my cell. I heard someone yell, "Throw it all out, Sam!"

I looked out and saw that the stuff was coming from a cell across from me and up one tier. Two officers then showed up. They were the goon squad. One of them, Big Bill, was about 6'4" and I'd say that he hit the scales at about 250 pounds. The other one was Arizona Jim and he was about 6' and he weighed around 235. Sam was a Native American. Big Bill told Sam to come out, he was going to the TU.

"Come in and get me!" Sam yelled.

Big Bill started into the cell, but Sam was ready and when he hit Big Bill, he knocked him back out the door! Big Bill looked at Arizona Jim and asked, "You want to try?"

Well Jim went in, and Sam knocked him to his knees. The cell door was so narrow that only one big guard at a time could go through it. Sam knew that, so he'd brace himself and hit them when they rushed in. He had those two guards bloodied up pretty good. They finally just stood there, wondering what to do next. They didn't hear Lt. Mitchell, a guard the inmates called *Blue Boy*, come up. Lt. Mitchell ran Alcatraz. He was 5'11" and weighed somewhere around 350 pounds. Most people thought Blue Boy was fat, but I was to see on my first day on the Rock that Lt. Mitchell was definitely not fat.

He stopped right in front of my cell. He ordered the two officers to come down. They came down and he said to them, "One tough Indian, huh?" Then Blue Boy went up on the tier and looked in Sam's cell.

"All right Sam," he said, "You've had your fun. Come on, we're going to the TU. You put on a good show for the new boys, but now it's time to take your punishment like a man."

Sam asked Blue Boy if he was planning on taking him all by himself. Blue Boy nodded.

"Well, come on in," Sam said, "I've been waiting for you!"

That was Sam's mistake. After that, it was over so quickly I could hardly believe my eyes. Blue Boy went in that door so fast, body-slammed Sam on the way in and carried him into the back wall. There he put an arm lock on him, turned him around and propelled him out the door with a kick in the rear end.

He put a boot in Sam's pants every step down the tier. Believe me when I said Sam went to the TU! We learned right away that Blue Boy was certainly no one to fool with, but in all my four years on the Rock, I found him to be the fairest officer that I ever had any dealings with. If you had a break coming, he gave you one. If you wanted to be a tough guy, he'd give it to you that way too. After all of the excitement had calmed down, I lay on my bunk wondering what kind of a place I had gotten myself into. As it turned out, this incident was just the first of a long list of crazy things that I witnessed happening on that island.

The next day, we got *processed*. The doctor gave us a physical, we met the warden and we were read the list of *do's and don'ts* from Blue Boy, Lt. Mitchell. He also let us know that we would be assigned a job and we'd be required to work at that job for six months before we could apply for a different one. We weren't allowed to go to the yard for the first two weeks, the reason being that we were still on fish row. That first weekend at Alcatraz was the longest two days of my life. The only time that we were allowed out of our cells was at mealtimes, for about thirty minutes at a time.

The following Monday, the cell house lieutenant came by and gave each of us a slip. My slip said that I was assigned to work in the kitchen. One of the inmates who had ridden on the train with me was assigned to the kitchen too. Neither of us was happy about it. However, the rule book was clear: if you refused to work, you got six months in the TU. I really did not want to begin my stay on the Rock by doing six months in the Treatment Unit though, so I decided to give it a try. The next day I was moved to cell 127. I didn't care much for that either, as there were inmates in the cells directly across from me, which meant that I would have no privacy whatsoever.

The kitchen turned out to be a very easy and good job. There were four of us assigned to wipe down the tables and benches after each meal. After the evening meal, we also had to sweep and mop the floors. When our work was done, we could sit and drink coffee and even snack on pastry if we could sneak some out of the bakery. A big factor that made the job pleasant was that we got to shower daily and we were issued clean white clothes each day. We got extra food and coffee too, anytime we wanted it. I worked in the dining room for a couple of months. After that, I got the job of making the coffee and preparing the other drinks. Then I moved up to *salad man*. I became very good friends then with one of the dinner cooks, who really knew how to prepare good food. He had been a chef on a Madison Lines ship called *The Lorelei,* a luxury liner that sailed all over the world. I learned a lot about food preparation from him, and when he got transferred, I took his job.

The food on Alcatraz was good. The menu changed all of the time and there was always a variety of food to fix. Unlike the other prisons that I had been in, there was no commissary on the island. In the other places you could buy packaged candy, cookies, fresh fruit and ice cream. At Alcatraz, everything that you ate came out of the kitchen. Holidays on the Rock were always occasions for great meals. Christmas and Thanksgiving consisted of turkey with all the trimmings, right down to the fresh pumpkin pie. At New Year's and on the Fourth of July, we had T-bone steaks. The vegetables were always fresh because the chief steward went shopping at the produce market in San Francisco five days a week. Every once in awhile, he brought back fresh fruit. Every other month or so we would make candy, which was always a big hit.

The dinner cooks were allowed a certain amount of ingredients for a meal, and if we didn't use them all we stored them, and then we traded them to the chief steward for meat, which we used to make a *chef's meal.* Whenever the inmates saw *chef's meal* on the menu board, they knew that they were in for a special dinner. We usually had a chef's meal about once every three months.

Very rarely, there would be a bad meal, and when

there was, it hit the walls, the ceilings, the floors and even the unfortunate officers who were pulling mess hall duty. Whenever that happened, someone wound up in TU. Some of the really special meals that I remember were when the striped bass were running in the Bay. The officers caught them by the wheelbarrow load and rolled them to the kitchen. The cooks cleaned and cooked them and the inmates got all of the fish that they could eat. We would stuff the small ones, the one to two pounders, with a nice gumbo and bake them. The bigger ones were cut into steaks and fried. The bass run would last about a month and since Friday was traditionally *fish day*, we could have four or five of these delicious meals.

When Warden Blackwell took over the prison he made quite a few changes. For the first time we had hot water in the cells. That was a real treat! We didn't have to shave in cold water any more. Also, he put in spring bunks with new mattresses which was a major improvement. No more slat bunks. He also approved musical instruments. If you had money on the books you could buy one. We were allowed one hour each evening to play. He approved a Saturday practice time, so we could put together a band. The band was allowed to play in the mess hall on holidays. I knew how to play the harmonica, so I bought a couple of them in different keys. I also bought a guitar and learned how to play it. There was an inmate who at one time had been a high school music teacher. He helped a lot of the other guys learning to play different instruments and as a result, we came up with a pretty fair band and it helped to pass the time.

Another thing that Warden Blackwell did, was to make it possible for the inmates who worked in the kitchen to earn some extra money as well as to earn some extra good time. All other federal institutions have what is called *meritorious good time* and *meritorious pay.* I worked in the kitchen all of the time that I was on Alcatraz and I think that it was two years after I arrived, in 1961, that I started getting meritorious good time and pay. I got paid $35.00 a month and two extra days a month good time. I was very unhappy when I was first informed that I would be working in the kitchen. I didn't know any better, being a newcomer to Alcatraz. Later I realized what a great assignment the kitchen really was. As far as I was concerned, I had the best job on the island.

A really big benefit was escaping that sixteen hours in your cell every day. Those cells were only five feet wide and nine feet long. The small area was very confining and it seemed even smaller than the actual size really was as the time went by. That was what really seemed to get to most of the inmates, the fact that you were in such an enclosed area day after day. I was confined to the area of the kitchen, cell house and a limited exercise yard. In four years, they seemed to get smaller and smaller.

The inmates who worked in the dish and dining rooms had to work only about an hour after each of the meals. After shower time in the morning, they were allowed to go to the yard. When I became a dinner cook, I worked every other day. The shifts rotated, so one day I worked the evening meal and the next day I worked the morning and noon meal. That meant a great deal to me because even on my time off I could go to the kitchen and also go to the yard. You can ask any inmate who served time on Alcatraz, and he will tell you that being able to escape that sixteen hours in his cell was a real benefit. My first year on Alcatraz was not a pleasant time. No time in prison is enjoyable, but after that first year of getting used to the system there, that island really began to close in on me.

Being in the same enclosed area day after day affected people in different ways. Some simply went crazy. Others lashed out in anger and went to the Treatment Unit just to have a change in their surroundings. Others took college courses to occupy their minds. Some, like the famous bird man, had hobbies. I had three things that always kept me on my toes. The first one was staying out of trouble and keeping alive. The second was trying to maintain my sanity. The third was to keep from being involved with homosexual activities.

Homosexuality is a real problem in all prisons, but at Alcatraz we all had our own individual cells, so it wasn't quite as prevalent. Still, it existed. One very bad incident that I remember happening took place in the dish room in the kitchen. There was a big fellow who liked to throw his weight around, and he wasn't very well liked by most of the other inmates. He had been trying to force himself on some of the slighter inmates, who of course didn't like it. One of those smaller inmates tried his best to avoid the bully, but it was impossible as they both worked in the dish room. On the advice of the other inmates who were also being harassed by the same man, the little guy looked around for something to knock the bully's brains out and came up with a big brass pipe that he found inside the dishwasher.

He unscrewed the pipe and decided to lay in wait for his tormentor. He was in the dish room when the big guy came in from the yard. I was in the kitchen preparing the noon meal when I heard some commotion coming from the other room, but I didn't pay much attention to it. Then several of the guys that worked in there came out and hurried into the dining room. After a few seconds the officer on duty came on the run. He ran right back out and went to the telephone. Then he blew a whistle and made us all go into the dining room. The goon squad rushed past us and took the guy out on a stretcher to the prison hospital and later they transferred him to the federal medical institution at Springfield, Missouri where he died two days later. The general consensus of all of the inmates was that he got what he deserved.

We heard later that the little inmate had done a good job. He had completely knocked one of the big man's eyes out and he had given him a nineteen inch skull fracture. The warden and Blue Boy grilled us all separately but no one said a word. We had heard and seen nothing. I believe that they knew who did it, and they also knew that we all knew, but no one ratted on the little guy. They never did arrest anyone. The reason that they couldn't get any information on the killing was due to the **Inmate Code** that the inmates on Alcatraz lived by. If someone got killed, we protected the guy who lived as there is nothing you can do for the one who gets killed. He's already dead, so we protect the other guy so that he doesn't have to go to court and get more time.

One other similar incident that I remember took place in the shower room. The shower room was just a big open room with drains in the floor and pipes overhead with shower heads spaced every so often on the pipes. It was a community shower room so a lot of inmates showered together. The guards stood at the door controlling groups of men who entered and left. The two inmates involved in the fight worked in the same shop in one of the prison industry factories. The bigger con had been repeatedly trying to force himself on the smaller one in one of the bathroom stalls. The little guy decided that he had taken enough. He made arrangements with another inmate who worked in the shower room issuing clean clothes, to slip him a knife. When the big inmate was in the shower all soaped up, the little guy went up behind him and stabbed him in the back. The knife broke off in the big guy's spine. That's all there was to the fight. Several of the officers saw what happened and the little inmate was quickly arrested and taken to the Treatment Unit. The stabbed inmate also went to the medical center at Springfield, and word got back to us that he was paralyzed from the waist down. A later rumor had it that he got into another confrontation there and someone else did kill him. On Alcatraz, one of the rules that should be noted was that, even if an inmate was declared dead, the officers could not take his body off of the island unless it was handcuffed and shackled. Why, I can't tell you, but it was a rule and it was carried out.

A few days after this fight, I was in the kitchen working when the officer on duty told me to report to the cell house lieutenant. I had no idea what was going on as I hadn't done anything wrong. I reported as ordered and there was an attorney there who informed me that I was going to be a witness for the accused inmate. In fact, I was one of fifteen inmates who had *volunteered* to take the stand on the inmate's behalf! On the day of his trial, we were taken across the Bay to the federal court in San Francisco. The attorney called us each up to the stand in turn and asked us if the accused had acted in self-defense. Every one of us swore that he had. As a result, the jury found him not guilty by reason of self-defense. The **Inmate Code** had withstood another test.

Another code that the inmates lived by was to warn a fellow inmate if an officer was walking the tier. The reason behind this was that if you were doing something that you weren't supposed to be doing, you had enough time to stop, for when you were in your cell, you couldn't see or hear an officer approaching. The only way we had of looking down the tier was by sticking a shaving mirror out of the bars and then to look in it. My one and only experience with the dreaded Treatment Unit was when I got caught carrying a knife.

I had just come in from work and sat down on my bunk. Like almost every other inmate, I carried a small knife down in my sock for protection. I had gotten it from one of the guys who worked in one of the shops and the beauty of it was that it was made of brass, so I could carry it through the metal detectors without setting them off. As it happened, I had the last cell on flats just before what was known as *the cutoff*. This was the corner of the tier and if an officer came from that direction there was no time to detect him. Sure enough, it was my bad luck that day that an officer approached from that direction. He asked what I had and of course I replied that I had nothing. Then he asked why I jumped when he came around the corner. I told him that he had scared me.

"I scared you all right," he said, "Because you have something that you shouldn't have!"

He signaled the cell house guard at the desk to open cell 127. He ordered me to step outside and put my hands on the bars. I did as I was told and he pulled up my pant leg and found the knife. The standing rule for carrying a weapon was thirty days in the Treatment Unit. The first three days that I was in the TU, I spent in the hole. All that I can say about it is that it was cold and black. I was in a cell with four walls, but it was so dark that I couldn't see the ceiling or the floor. There was a hole in the floor that served as the toilet. If I needed water, I had to ask the guard who turned it on from the outside. The next twenty-seven days I spent in a regular cell that was in the same place and the only difference was that I had a mattress to sleep on. I was really glad when those thirty days were over.

Beer making on Alcatraz was always a lot of fun. The ingredients were easy to get and we could always count on the inmates who worked in the bakery to get yeast for us. We would stir up a big batch in the kitchen, pour it into jars that we saved for just that purpose and then hide it all over the place. We always hoped that the stewards wouldn't find all of it. When they did, they would pour it out in front of us. It was no big deal though. We just made more.

There was one steward who really seemed to have a nose for the stuff and he could smell that brew a mile away. It really tickled him to find a jar and pour it out while we watched. What a waste! He was so good that we were having a hard time keeping enough hidden so that it had time to ferment. Out of the eight jars that we made at one time, maybe two or three would make it through. Another guard had the nasty habit of urinating in our jars and then putting them back. After awhile though, we finally found a place to hide it and no one ever found it again.

The chief steward had a glassed-in office right in the middle of the kitchen. There was a big copper fire extinguisher hanging right on the side of his office wall. It was one of the ancient kind that you had to turn upside down when you used it. It held four gallons. We took out all of the insides and polished it up real nice. We got ready for the first batch. We mixed up the ingredients and poured them into our new receptacle. We had carefully plugged the hose so that no smells could escape. We didn't want that bird- dog steward sniffing around! Every other day, on the pretense of polishing it, we would take it down to the basement and let the gas buildup out. Next we hid a few jars in some obvious places just to throw the stewards off of our trail and to keep them from becoming suspicious, which they would have done if suddenly they did-n't find any. That fire extinguisher was still hanging there on the day that I departed from Alcatraz and in fact, I'm sure that there was a batch brewing in it when the island closed.

Friday afternoon was our beer time. We would go into the bakery one or two at a time and have ourselves a little drink. Every once in awhile someone would have a little too much and not be able to make it back to his cell. He'd get caught in the shakedown leaving the kitchen and they'd haul him away to the Treatment Unit. The standing rule for getting drunk was five days in the TU.

Just about the time he'd get out, another batch would be ready.

I was lucky and never got caught. I know though that the officer in the kitchen had to be suspicious on Friday afternoons with so much traffic going in and coming out of the bakery. The stewards knew what was going on but they just looked the other way. Once they had us trained they really didn't want to lose us. In fact, there were a lot of the custody officers that just looked the other way too, as long as nobody was getting hurt. All of the inmates knew who those officers were and we never took advantage of them.

There were even officers who would bring things for certain inmates. No hacksaw blades or guns or anything of that nature, but an extra pack of cigarettes, or fresh fruit, or maybe a candy bar. This was always greatly appreciated by the inmates and no way would anyone take advantage of these officers. Those types of items were ones that an inmate didn't get very often and sometimes not at all. At Alcatraz, there was very little trouble between the officers and the inmates. The trouble was most always between the incarcerated men.

Another code observed among the inmates was that when a prisoner was talking to an officer, he stood back and spoke in a very loud voice so that everybody nearby could hear what was being said. This was to ensure that you were not known as a snitch. If you got a reputation as a snitch, you had a tough row to hoe. Many such people ended up dead. Other inmates were known as **solid cons.** These inmates could be trusted not to tell anything they knew, no matter what might happen to them. As for myself, I was considered to be a solid con. I was trusted not to reveal anything. When John Anglin approached me one Saturday in the yard, he was aware of my reputation. I knew him from Leavenworth and we had worked together in the kitchen on the island. He wanted to know if I'd go out on a limb and help him and his brother get some tools. I thought about it for a few minutes and then I told him that I could do that. He asked me to break things in the kitchen if I had to, and then the inmates on the maintenance crew would leave tools behind when they finished working in the kitchen. Then, using a waste pipe, I'd lower it to him in the room below. I told him I'd be glad to help him.

I knew of course, that an escape plan was underway. The particulars I did not know, and I sure wasn't asking any questions. The following week the maintenance crew came into the kitchen to do some work. An inmate on the crew came up to me and slipped me a screwdriver.

"This is for John," he said. "Send it down the pipe at two o'clock straight up!"

At two o'clock I went to the restroom and unscrewed the cap on the four-inch waste line. I tied a heavy cord to the screwdriver and started lowering it. I heard a tap on the pipe so I knew that John was waiting. When I felt a couple of short jerks on the cord, I pulled it up and put the cap back on the line. A few days later, the same inmate passed me a pair of channel locks with the same message. This went on for several months and suddenly it ceased. I found out later that I was just one of the many sources from whom they were collecting tools.

Another day, out in the yard, John asked me if I had a raincoat. Some of the inmates had one and others didn't. I said that I did. He said that the next time that it looked like rain to wear it to the yard. A few days later it did rain, so I wore it and when yard time was over, John wore it out. I knew then that they had a well-thought out plan in the works.

It was of course, the escape attempt made famous in the movie *Escape from Alcatraz* with Clint Eastwood. One of the tools that I had sent down the pipe to John was a pair of scissors. They had made dummy heads and added real hair to make them look realistic. Every night at music hour, the three men put the dummy heads in their bunks and then they climbed up the pipes in the back of their cells and went to work cutting the bars on the vent that they went out of. The music hours served as a cover for the noise that they made. They worked for months cutting those bars because they didn't have any good cutting tools. They made a rubber raft out of our raincoats as well as some life jackets. They spent hours figuring out every detail.

The main element that they took care to calculate was the *time* element. That was the factor that would determine the success or failure of the operation. No one knows at just what time they put those dummies in their bunks, but I would bet that they went out right after lights-out on June 11, 1962. If my guess is right, they had from 10.30 p.m. on June 11, until the morning of June 12 at 7:30 a.m. when they were discovered missing. At the standing count that morning the guards found the heads and immediately the whole island was locked down. It stayed that way for two full days. The FBI came in and questioned each and every one of us, but as usual, none of us knew a thing about it. In retaliation, the officers tore up a lot of cells over the following weeks. The inmates would come in from work and their cells would have been tossed, with stuff lying all over. Rumors started flying that the authorities were thinking of closing Alcatraz and that the officers were trying to provoke a riot to keep it afloat or still operational. The food got worse with the chief steward cutting back on the good meals.

One of the questions that I'm always asked by visitors to the island is, do I think the Anglin brothers made it off the island?

I think so. Those boys grew up in the Everglades in Florida and I think they went back there and disappeared.

Things were just starting to quiet down after the escape by Frankie Morris and the Anglin brothers, when there was another attempt, this time by two guys known as Scott and Parker. You didn't hear much about this escape because they knew for sure that Scott had actually

Darwin sharing his stories with Alcatraz visitors.

made it to the mainland. He landed on the rocks, just below the sea wall at a place called Fort Mason. He was badly spent from the swim across the Bay and the rocks had cut up his legs pretty severely. There were some children playing along the wall and they spotted Scott down on the rocks. He was lying there trying to catch his breath and get himself together. The kids went to the post entrance and reported him to the MPs on duty. They in turn radioed the Army tugboat which went around and fished Scott off of his rocky ledge. They took him to the post hospital, not knowing who he was.

They had just left him there when the escape whistle

Darwin with a visitor on Alcatraz.

on Alcatraz blew. On the two-way radio they learned that there had been an escape so they called the island and asked for a description of the man. Of course, Scott matched the description and then they notified the warden about the person that they had found lying on the rocks. The officers from the island immediately went to the post hospital and picked him up.

I had been in the kitchen working when it was discovered that two inmates were missing. They sent us to our cells and conducted a standing count to determine for certain who was gone. The escape whistle went off, and just a short time later they brought Parker down Broadway in his birthday suit. They took him directly to

Darwin visits his cell #127 on "Broadway."

the Treatment Unit and threw him in. It turned out that the poor guy had jumped into the Bay and he didn't even know how to swim. The current had carried him out to what was known as *Little Alcatraz* which is just a rock that sticks up out of the water about sixty yards from the island itself. He just huddled on that promontory until the officers came and picked him up. Warden Blackwell went over himself to bring Scott back. He was marched down Broadway stark naked as well, except for the bandages on his legs where he had been flailed about on the rocks. Scott and Parker got five years added to their sentences for their botched effort.

A few days later we heard rumors again that Alcatraz was getting shut down, only this time they turned out to be true. In just a matter of weeks the first chain of thirty men were taken off the island. Men were eventually sent to just about every federal institution that there was in the federal prison system. It took the last month of 1962 as well as the first two of 1963, to phase out all of the inmates. They put them on a federal immigration plane that carried thirty at a time. I was in one of the last groups to board that plane and I left the island in February of 1963.

They flew me back to the federal penitentiary at Leavenworth where I was to remain for a little over a year.

After my second year on the Rock, I began to realize that unless something happened I'd be spending the rest of my life behind bars. I was twenty-eight years old with a sentence of eighty years, which put me at the end of my sentence in the year 2038. It didn't take a mathematician to figure out that I wasn't going to live long enough to serve out my sentence.

The majority of the cons on Alcatraz were serving time for bank robbery. I kept hearing about a jailhouse attorney who knew the laws concerning bank robbery, inside out. A friend of mine encouraged me to talk to him to see if my conviction was flawed. He agreed to introduce me to him, so we went to the exercise yard that weekend and I met Courtney Taylor. Courtney was the only man to be on the FBI's *Most Wanted List* for a non-violent crime. Courtney was a master forger.

He was a portly old man and he looked like he should be in a business suit instead of the convict garb that he was wearing. Right off he started asking me questions about my sentence, and how much time I was serving. Within a very few minutes he told me that he could almost certainly get me a reduction in my sentence. He said that bank robbery convictions all had to run concurrently, not consecutively. He told me that the seventy years that I received on the bank robbery charge had to be reduced to twenty years. Boy did that sound good to me!

He told me to send for my court papers and to come see him again when they arrived. The very next weekend, with them in hand, I went to see Courtney again. He told me that he would write me up a motion and bring it to me in about a week. He was as good as his word and he brought me the motion the next weekend, and I put it in the mail the following Monday.

It took about six weeks before I got a reply from the Court. Courtney was right! The Court corrected the sen-

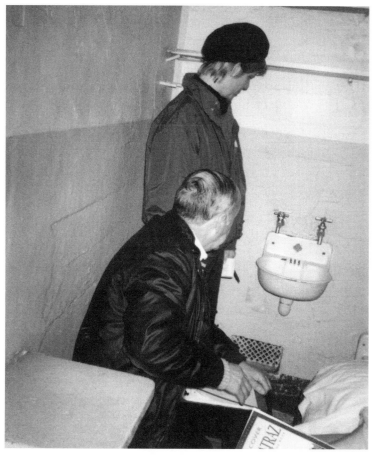

Darwin with visitor inside cell #127.

tence and ran all the sentences on the bank robbery concurrently, which cut my sentence from eighty years to a
total of thirty years (twenty years on the robbery charges,
plus ten more on the two escape charges). I took the papers to the yard and then Courtney gave me some really
good news: he told me that the twenty year sentence that

I had on the bank robbery wasn't valid and that they would have to vacate it completely. He told me that he would write me a brief but not to file it until after the five year statute of limitations had run out.

The statute of limitations ran out in 1963 and Courtney was right again. I filed the motion after Alcatraz closed and I was back in Leavenworth. Like he said, the Court had to vacate the bank robbery sentence in its entirety. The bad part was that I was indicted by a Grand Jury and I was returned to Sioux City for a new trial on section 2113e of the Federal Bank Robbery Statute. To explain why I was taken back to Sioux City, Iowa for a new trial, I have to go back to 1958.

When we were arrested, we were charged with violation of the Federal Bank Robbery Statute, sections 2113a, 2113b, 2113d, and 2113e. We attempted to escape out of the Woodbury County Jail and for our efforts we got two additional charges—attempted escape and assault on a federal officer. The fourth bank robbery charge, under 2113e, for forcing the bank manager to go with me to the bank, carried a minimum sentence of ten years, and a maximum sentence of death! We pled guilty and received a grand total of eighty years. But because Section 2113e is a capital crime, those charges had to be brought by a grand jury indictment. The government made the mistake of bringing the charges against us based on a United States attorney's information. By not indicting us by a grand jury, all of the sentences on the bank robbery statutes were illegal because the Court did not even have the authority to hear the case without a grand jury indictment! Therefore, they were all vacated, which left me with a legal sentence of ten years on the separate charges for escape and assaulting a federal officer. After serving the ten year sentence, less good time, I had to be released. By reducing the 10 years with statutory good time @ 10 days per month or 1,200 days plus 217 days extra good, earned both in working in Prison Industries and receiving meritorious good time on Alcatraz, my new release date became 11/12/64.

I waited five years before bringing the motion to vacate Courtney Taylor wrote for me, like he said. But, apparently, the statute only ran on the first three bank robbery charges, because after the bank robbery sentences were vacated, much to my dismay, on 1/17/64 I received the bad news. The Grand Jury for the Northern District of Iowa returned an indictment, in Case 64-CR-3003-W, charging me with violation of Title 18 and 2113(e) (Bank robbery with a kidnapping).

On 11/12/64 I was released on Mandatory Release on the escape charges, and taken into custody by U.S. Marshals to return to Sioux City, Iowa to stand trail on Case No. 64-CR-3003-W.

I was in the Woodbury County Jail in Sioux City, Iowa 8 months waiting on several pre-trial motions to be heard. They were denied and I had a jury trial in which I was found guilty and on 5/20/65 I was sentenced to a new term of 20 years, under a new sentencing provision.

But, they made a mistake again! The new sentencing provision was a new law that had been passed which allowed a judge the option of letting a man sentenced under that provision to be eligible for parole at any time. But, section 2113e had a mandatory minium sentence of 10 years, so that new sentencing provision did not apply.

On 6/16/1966 I filed a motion with the Court to vacate and set aside the 20 years sentence I had received on Case 64-CR-3003-W on 5/20/1965. On 8/1/1966 the court issued an order vacating the 20 year sentence I had received on 5/20/1965, and issued an order for me to be returned to Sioux City, Iowa on 8/17/1966 to appear before the Court. I was returned to Sioux City, Iowa on 8/17/1966. Upon my return to the Court, after some 8 years, 6 months, I was finally given the first legal sentence for the Bank Robbery which took place in 1958, ten years, straight time. I served the sentence, less my good time, and I was released on November 17, 1972. That was a very joyous day for me! I had served a total of 14 years, 7 months and 23 days. I am glad to say that since then I have never violated any law, state or federal, and I never will.

Following is a list of dates and actions taken by the Court:

1958   Charged on US Attorney's Information
           2113a, 2113b, 2113d, 2113e, assault on Federal
           Offices, attempted escape
           Sentenced   2113a, 20 years
                           2113b, 10 years
                           2113d, 20 years
                           2113e, 20 years
           Assault on Federal Offices, 5 years
           Attempted escape, 5 years

1963   Bank Robbery, 2113a, 2113b, 2113d, 2113e, sentences vacated

1963   Released—served time on sentences for assault on Federal Offices and attempted escape.

1963   Returned to Sioux City, Iowa to stand trial for 2113e

1964   Trial by jury. Found guilty of 2113e, sentenced to 20 years under A number

1964   Returned to Federal Penitentiary, Leavenworth, Kansas

1965   Sentence vacated under 2113e (A number)

1965   Returned to Sioux City, Iowa for re-sentencing on 2113e, sentenced to 10 years

1972   Released under mandatory release time served less good time.

While I was serving time on the Rock, one of my sisters was living in Oakland. She came to see me quite often. One weekend she came to visit, bringing her daughter and her little grandchild with her. When they had arrived at the boat dock before crossing to the island, the boat captain informed them that no children were allowed on Alcatraz. This upset my sister and she let the captain know it! However, he was polite to her and he told her that he had to abide by the rules. The only one who could give her permission was the warden. Well, my sister called the warden and when she told him who she was coming to visit, he remembered me from the officer's dining room and he said, "Oh you mean Darwin? He's a great cook! Sure you can bring the baby over!"

That baby, my great-niece, was the only child ever permitted to visit an inmate in the history of Alcatraz.

Freedom

After being released in November of 1972, I was very happy to be a free man, but my troubles were far from over. I had promised myself that I would never put myself in the position where I could be sent back to prison. The four years that I had served on Alcatraz had made a believer out of me. I vowed never again to break the law. I needed to find a job and to become a productive citizen. This is where the problems began. How does a man apply for a job? Every application you fill out you have to lie about something. If you answer *yes* to the question *Have you ever committed a felony?* your chances of getting hired are zero. Then the application wants to know where you have previously worked. How do you explain that you have been in prison for the last fifteen years?

I had made a considerable amount of money while I was in prison, so I didn't have to worry about money right away. However, I got so tired of trying to live a lie that I turned to alcohol and tried to hide in a bottle. I was a great success at drinking, because as a real live alcoholic, I would have blackouts and not remember what I had done the day before. This began to scare me, so when an old friend of mine that I had gone to school with suggested that I get help, I did. I now thank the Lord for such a good friend. That friend not only came to see me while I was in treatment, but he went out on a limb and gave me a job when I got out. He had a lot of rental property and I did maintenance work for him.

I managed to get my life straightened up and I began going to church. The only people in the church who knew about my past were the pastor and his wife. The only reason that I confided in the pastor was because he too, as a young man, had had trouble with alcohol and a brush with the law.

I had been attending church services for about a year, when one Sunday morning the pastor announced that we had a guest speaker. He was a man about forty years old. He started speaking and I found myself listening very intently. He was telling my story! He too had been a bank robber and he spoke of many instances that were similar to my own past history. I took in every word that he had to say. When the service was over, I approached him at the back of the church.

I introduced myself and the first question out of my mouth was, "How can you stand up in front of all these people and tell the story that you just told?"

He looked me straight in the eye and said, "I'm not the same person who did all of those horrible things."

Well, I guess that I must have looked at him sort of funny.

He said, "Do you know Jesus?"

I told him that I believed in God. He replied that he had accepted Jesus as his personal savior and he no longer had to carry all of those sins anymore. I wasn't quite sure what he meant, but he said, "Come with me and let's talk with your pastor." He went up to the pastor and murmured something to him. The pastor turned to me and said, "You are long overdue."

The three of us went into the pastor's office and the two of them started in on me. I didn't know much about the Bible, but they began explaining in very simple terms that I needed a personal relationship with Jesus. The pastor told me not to worry about it, he would explain everything to me in due time. The following week the pastor stopped by my house several times and each time he spoke about my need to have a deeper relationship with Christ. The following Sunday morning at the end of the service, the pastor made an altar call. The next thing I knew I was standing in front of him and he was praying over me. On that day, I became reborn.

A few weeks later, I got a call from the guest speaker who had been at our church.

He said, "I hear that you accepted Jesus as your personal savior."

I told him that I had. Then he asked me if I would go with him to Springfield, South Dakota to a church and be a witness for the Lord. I asked him what all that would entail and he said, " All you have to do is tell your story."

I told him that I didn't think that I could do that.

He said, "Sure you can! I need you really badly. Chuck Colson's prison fellowship has permission to go into the prison there and I need to get some people who will volunteer to go in with us."

Well, we got some people and we went into the prison. It was to be a three-day seminar. It began on a Friday evening and there were about eighty inmates waiting for us. My friend, the speaker, whose name was Bill, started things off, explaining why we were there. Then he said to the cons that he had someone with him who all of them could relate to. He introduced me and when I stood up in front of those eighty inmates, the first thing that came to my mind was how lucky I was, because when the service was over, I could go home.

I stood there for a few moments wondering how I should start.

Darwin at the store he ran for the church in Iowa.

I said, "There are about eighty people sitting right here in front of me and every one of you are wishing that you were what I am. I'm an ex-con."

Well, every one of those inmates got to their feet and I thought that they would never stop clapping. It's funny how people relate to their own kind. They knew that I had been there too. We went back on Saturday and Sunday and on both days I tried to shake hands with every one of them. One night, a Native American who was in the group came up to me and we had a long talk. Later, as we were leaving, one of the guards came over to me and told me that the man had been there for four years and that I was the only person that he'd ever spoken to.

I was astounded and I said, " No kidding!"

The guard said, " No kidding. In fact we all call him 'Silent Joe.'"

The last day that we were there, on Sunday, Bill gave an altar call. Silent Joe stood up on his chair and hollered, "If Darwin believes in God, then so do I!" He then jumped off the chair, ran down in front and fell to his knees in front of the altar.

I went over and put my hands on his shoulders and said, "God bless you, Joe."

We started a Bible study class there that met once a month. I conducted that class for two and a half years and never missed a class. Many of the inmates, upon release, called me and many of them still in prison, wrote to me weekly. It gave me a very good feeling to know that those inmates looked forward to our coming each month.

Many of them told me, "We appreciate you people because you come to see us each month out of the goodness of your hearts and not for money. You care about us."

I changed jobs and had to move away and I really missed going to see those guys. Before I left, the warden who was a woman, called us in for a meeting. She told us that since we had established the prison ministry, the problems inside with the inmates had been diminished to the point where there was almost no trouble at all anymore. We were glad to hear that. It was my reward for time well spent.

One night, some time later, my wife Marge and I were watching television when our pastor called and asked if we could come over to his house. We went right over, and there he told us about a young girl who needed a place to stay. She was in treatment for drugs and alcohol abuse, but was ready to be released. Her family did not want her and none of them would give her a place to stay. Then he asked if we would be willing to take her in. I told him that I would be glad to, but the decision was up to my wife. My wife asked if we could meet with her before giving a final answer. The pastor replied that that was why he had asked us over. The treatment center was just a few blocks away and we could go right then.

I was surprised at how young the girl looked. She was only fifteen years old. She was very pretty and also very polite. We sat and talked for awhile and I could see that Marge was going to say *yes*. I asked the pastor then if he and I could have a few minutes in private. When we were out of earshot, I told the pastor that I wanted my wife to talk with her alone. He said that he understood. When we came back, Marge and the girl were sitting side-by-side, holding each other's hands. I could see that there had been a few tears shed. I asked Marge what she thought and she said that we were going to take the young girl home with us. So we did. We took her home and what a joy she turned out to be!

While she was staying with us, we realized that we had not been legally authorized to care for her, so I con-

Twenty-one room house in Iowa, re-modeled by Darwin, where he and his wife raised nine foster children.

Darwin and his wife Marge with their foster children in the 1970s.

Darwin's foster children, early '80s.

Darwin and family, 1980.

tacted a friend that I had in Child Protective Services. I explained the situation, that she was a minor, and that we didn't want her family to cause us any trouble. He told us that we should come down to his office and sign up to be foster parents. The following day we did just that. We underwent the training that was required and a whole new life opened up for us. In the following years we had ninety-four different children come to live in our home. Some stayed with us for years, and others, for just a short time. Child Protective Services made our home into what is called a *safe house*. At one time we had nine children living with us over the Christmas season.

The first children that we received from the State of Iowa, where we were living at the time, were two babies. They were half-sisters, just eleven months apart. The oldest was sixteen months and the youngest, five months. They had really been neglected. They dropped them off in the morning and told us to take them to the doctor right away. They both needed a bath and we didn't have any clean clothes for them. We sat down and made a list of all the things that we needed. While Marge bathed them, I went to the store for supplies.

When the doctor had seen both of the girls, she told us that the youngest was very underweight at only eight pounds and would have to go into the hospital. My wife stayed with her in the hospital for seven days and nights. In that time, the baby managed to gain three pounds, but even so the doctor told Marge not to blame herself if the

Darwin and his sister Harriet.

little girl died. It certainly would not be her fault. Finally, they let us take her home. Marge got a little doll bed out of the closet and put it on the night stand next to our bed. She fed that little girl every two hours around the clock. Every day you could see that she was getting better. She grew up to become a very beautiful girl.

We also received another little girl that was a half-sister to the two that we had. Child Protective Services took her from the mother just after she was born. We had three little girls, all from the same mother, but from three different fathers. We raised them as if they were our very own and we even tried to adopt them, but we were turned down because of our ages. It didn't matter though because we were the only parents that they ever knew and they still call me *Papa*.

Darwin at home with Tippy Two.

When I lost my wife a few years ago, I was alone in Iowa. All of my family were living out in California, so in 1994 I moved there too. I went to work for a large rental property company. In 1996 my legs gave out due to poor circulation. I had bypass surgery in December of 1996 and again in December of 1997. I still have one leg that isn't quite right, but I'm happy. I have the Lord and I have enough money to pay my bills, and really, that's all anyone really needs.

INTERESTING FACTS
ABOUT ALCATRAZ

The first warden of Alcatraz was James A. Johnson. He was warden from the first day that Alcatraz became a federal prison, on August 22, 1934. Warden Johnson retired in 1948. He died in 1958 at the age of eighty-two. The boat that was used to ferry people back and forth from Alcatraz was named the *Warden Johnson.*

The second warden of Alcatraz was Edwin B. Swope. He ruled the island with a firm hand. He did not believe in coddling convicted felons. He made a real enemy when he made Robert F. Stroud (the birdman of Alcatraz) send his extensive bird book collection home. Stroud resented him and swore that he'd get even with him one day. Of course he never did.

Warden Swope was replaced by the third warden of Alcatraz, Paul J. Madigan, on January 10, 1955. The cons nicknamed him *Promising Paul.* He had the habit of promising certain requests made by the cons but would never deliver.

The fourth and final warden was Olin G. Blackwell. The cons considered him to be a real-square shooter with a great sense of humor. I got to know Warden Blackwell from his frequent visits to the officers' dining room. He ate there fairly regularly and he always had a good word about the food. Blackwell ruled Alcatraz until the day that it closed. He had been warden of several other federal prisons before coming to the island. He died on March 7, 1986 at the age of seventy-one.

Alcatraz was a no-nonsense prison. You were there to serve your time and that was it. The guard ratio was one guard for every three inmates. Most federal prisons have a one to seven ratio. It was set up to see that every inmate was treated the same. There was no trustee system or any special privilege inmates. All inmates were subject to nightly cell shakedowns. The night shift lieutenant's hunch or whim would determine which cells would be thoroughly searched. Those unlucky inmates that were chosen were stripped naked and had to stand outside their cells while the guards searched through their belongings. They would look through every item and throw it on a pile on the floor, and run a metal detector over the mattress and pillow. If no contraband was found, the shakedown crew would leave to wreak havoc on yet another unfortunate inmate. This was typical of the daily harassment routine. If the shakedown crew found any contraband, the inmate was sent to the dreaded segregation unit in D Block.

Alcatraz guards who were assigned to the hellish D Block performed their duties with especially sadistic relish. The inmate that holds the record for time spent in D Block was Rufus "Whitey" Franklin. He was in isolation for seven straight years. It was punishment for killing a guard while trying to escape. At his trial he beat the gas chamber but received a life sentence to go along with the twenty-five years that he was already serving.

When an inmate would go over the edge and attack a guard he would attain instant respect and recognition from the other cons. On the other hand, if an inmate turned informant, he was labeled a *rat* and from that day on, he was ostracized and had no intimate friends. He was marked for death. Once labeled an informant that inmate didn't have much of a chance of surviving. His only hope was to go to Protective Custody. Protective Custody meant that that inmate would be locked away from the other cons. This being locked away was not altogether a sure-fire safe place. Many inmates went to lock-up and still wound up going out the back gate in a pine box.

In the famous riot and attempted escape of 1946, in which two guards were killed and fifteen others were wounded, three inmates were killed—Joe Cretzer, Marvin Hubbard and Barney Coy. They were considered the masterminds that plotted the ill-fated escape. Unable to get control of the situation, Warden Johnson called on the military. The Warden contacted two U.S. Army Generals, Frank Merill and Joe Stillwell who responded with eighty-four combat equipped marines who landed on Alcatraz. The marines bombarded the cell-house with bazookas and anti-tank shells. A hole was chopped in the cell-house roof and hand grenades and tear-gas bombs were dropped inside. Several hours after the marines had landed, the riot was over.

Numerous inmates were indicted for their parts in the riot. Myron Thompson and Sam Shockley received the death penalty and were executed in the San Quentin gas chamber. Nineteen year old Joe Carnes, Alcatraz's youngest inmate received a life sentence to go along with the one that he was already serving. Carnes was eventually granted a parole after serving thirty years. Joe was forty-seven years old when he was finally parolled. He died in 1994.

When you are free and rob banks, the hours are good, the pay is great, but the time that you get is a real bitch. I had been in a number of prisons before landing on the Rock. I had no idea how hard serving time could be until I was confined in the hell-hole called the Rock. I'm sure that every inmate who served time on Alcatraz had escape on his mind. I can tell you that escaping was always on *my* mind. Alcatraz is a twelve acre island and each day that you spend there, that island becomes smaller and smaller. Many of the inmates including myself, were sent to Alcatraz because we were deemed to be *escape minded.* We were considered incorrigibles, losers beyond redemption.

The total inmate population on the Rock averaged between two hundred and fifty to two hundred and sixty inmates. Whenever new inmates arrived on the Rock, the following day some lucky cons would be transferred to some other federal prison. Those lucky cons were getting close to being released or being eligible for parole. It was the policy of the Bureau of Prisons never to release any inmates from Alcatraz. The only exception to that rule was when an inmate was released by court order.

There were no gangs as such on Alcatraz. However, the black inmates had a section of the bleachers in the exercise yard that was their private domain. They would gather there and no other cons would intrude on their private turf.

When a fight broke out between two inmates, the fighting was always very fierce and no mercy was shown by either of the combatants. Of course, the onlookers would egg on the participants. The battle would rage until the guards arrived and separated the bloodied men. Both inmates would be taken to D Block for a thirty day cooling off period. A few of these guys, after being released from D Block, would pace the yard like wild beasts. These trouble-courting individuals with their tough-minded attitudes would sooner or later wind up right back in D Block. The Alcatraz rules were designed to drastically punish the rule breakers and rule breakers were in the minority. Most inmates learned to accept what they knew that they couldn't change.

There were no luxuries on Alcatraz. No newspapers or magazines. No commissary. The only things that the cons could purchase were painting supplies and the canvas to paint on. Later Warden Blackwell permitted musical instruments and sheet music. I played the harmonica and soon we used our practice time in our cells as a secret means of communication with each other, to warn when the guards were coming.

Every thing that you needed was furnished. You received two razor blades a week, one on Monday evening and one on Friday evening. Razor blades were exchanged with the guard, one for one. Soap was passed out every Wednesday, and you got a small bar as needed. It was a strong, foul-smelling soap, so there wasn't much demand for it. Tooth powder was exchanged on Wednesday evenings along with the soap. Again, exchange was made, one for one. You turned in an empty can to get a new one. You were given three packs of cigarettes each week, one on Monday evening, one on Wednesday evening, and one on Friday evening. You were allowed to have three packs in your cell. Anything over three packs were confiscated. I was lucky to have several friends who didn't smoke, so I made out great in that respect. You were issued three pairs of socks and it was up to you to keep them clean. You could exchange them pair for pair if you put in a request to the cell-house Lieutenant.

In 1955 when Madigan was the Warden, he had head-set earphone radios installed in the cells. You had two stations, one for sports and one for music, but there were no news programs of any kind allowed. Once a month they showed a movie, but few inmates went. There was a chapel but I do not remember any church services being held while I was on the Rock.

As far as its cells went, Alcatraz was no Hilton. Each cell had the following furnishings: A cot-sized bed made out of metal straps attached to an angel iron frame. It had two legs and the backside was attached to the wall. It had no springs and a very lumpy mattress with a matching pillow. You were given one sheet made out of a coarse material with a matching pillowcase, which you were allowed to exchange once a week. A thin army surplus blanket. A metal table, fastened to the wall, with an attached fold-down metal seat. A seat-less toilet, cold water sink and one tin drinking cup. Two wooden shelves on the rear wall above the sink and a wooden wall peg to hang your garments on. Believe me when I said it was no Hilton! Dimensions of each cell were five feet wide by nine feet long, by seven feet high. With all its elaborate furnishings, it made a man feel right at home!

Visitors were limited to the spouse, blood-relatives and attorneys. All visitors had to be pre-approved, and the same was true with all of the people to whom you corresponded. Anyone that you wrote to had to be pre-approved. Any visitors on your pre-approved list could visit you for two hours each month. You could receive unlimited incoming mail but you could write only five letters per month to each person on your pre-approved list. Visitors and inmates faced each other, separated by bullet-proof glass. You talked to each other through a telephone and conversations were closely monitored.

High above the cells, at the top of the building, were tall windows that were kept open winter and summer. Exactly fifteen minutes every night after lights out, like clockwork, one inmate, Andy Martinez, would yell, "Open the g.d. windows!"

No one could go to sleep until he had yelled it. Even the guards would wait for it. On rare occasions, when we'd all think that he'd forgotten, a few seconds later he'd yell, "Ha, ha, you guys thought I'd forgot! Close the g.d. windows!" It was one of the few things that all of us found amusing on the Rock.

The Great Audubon Caper

The inmates of Alcatraz demonstrated remarkable ingenuity and patience in their abilities to catch and even keep as pets, some of the various birds and small animals that were indigenous to the island. Some of the men also displayed wry senses of humor and marked talents for masterminding practical jokes on the gullible and to this day one that still stands out in my memory is the one that we dubbed *The Great Audubon Caper*.

The windows high up near the ceiling were open to the elements year round and sparrows, mostly, were frequent visitors inside the cell-house. The caper began when one was caught, probably inside the dining room looking for food tidbits, and one of the inmates who was working painting, dabbed it with a splash of color before letting it go. Perhaps he just wanted to be able to identify it if he saw it again.

At any rate, the idea quickly caught on and pretty soon more and more birds were appearing all over the island in a veritable rainbow of colors. Word about their fantastic plumage made it over to the San Francisco paper on the mainland and an article ran about the rare migrating species that must have been blown inland from an ocean storm and was sheltering on the island. Within a short time the Audubon Society had organized a day trip and we were inundated with another species, this one laden down with expensive cameras and other gear. Imagine their chagrin to find only ordinary sparrows and an occasional seagull covered in house paint and the inmates laughing at them.

The birds were numerous and they were always looking for something to eat. They were easy to catch by making a box snare. The inmate would make a box and prop up one edge with a small stick and tie a piece of string to the stick. They would sprinkle a few bread crumbs under the box and wait for one of the birds to come for the crumbs. Once they were under the box, it was just a matter of pulling the string and the box would drop down and trap the bird. Then they would paint the bird and turn it loose. Another rare species set free on the island!

The inmates were allowed to buy art supplies, including paint, so that's where they got all the different colors. This is also how they got the paint that was applied to the dummy heads used in the famous escape by Frankie Morris and the Anglin brothers.

Jo Jo the Mouse

Another little creature that always brightened up my day was a tiny brown mouse known as Jo Jo. He had been tamed by Rocky Medina, who was in the cell next to mine. Each day, barely a minute or two after I would arrive home in my cell after a full shift spent working in the kitchen, Jo Jo would materialize out of nowhere, his whiskers twitching and his bright beady eyes sparkling. Invariably, he would pause on his hind legs for a few moments, watching me, almost the way that a dog does, begging. I would carefully shake whatever crumbs that I had picked up from the bakery, out of my clothes for him and out of my pant-cuffs, especially for that is where most of them seemed to fall into. If I could, I would try frequently to bring him home some choice morsel as well.

One day, little Jo Jo appeared as usual, but I did a double take and then I couldn't stop laughing! The little

INTERESTING FACTS ABOUT ALCATRAZ

rodent was always such a gentleman, but this day Rocky, had exaggerated it by dressing him from neck to tail in a little mouse tuxedo, right down to a top hat!

Lizard Man

Another of the pets kept by one of the inmates was a small lizard. Sam worked at the garbage bin where the paper trash was burned each day. The job didn't require much time to complete, so Sam, a Native American, had plenty of time on his hands. One day he caught one of the many small lizards that lived on the island.

That little lizard became Sam's best friend. He carried it in his shirt pocket and took it with him every where he went. He had made it a collar out of a small piece of gold chain that he had found in the garbage and a leash out of some string. On week-ends he would take it to the recreation yard and let it run around on the sun-warmed concrete abutments that were actually the foundation to the main cell-house building.

One Saturday morning everyone was enjoying the bright sunshine, when all of a sudden, Sam erupted into a rage. At first, no one knew what had happened except that Sam was one mad Indian! He had had the lizard sunning itself when a seagull came down and snatched up the lizard, gold chain, string and all! He cussed that seagull for at least two full weeks. Every time he would think about it, he would start in again. Everyone felt sorry for Sam's loss, even the guards.

Alvin "Creepy" Karpis

When I finally reached the true end of the line and found myself on the Rock, there was an inmate there who had the misfortune of having served more time on Alcatraz than any other inmate. Alvin Karpis spent twenty-seven years on the Rock.

Karpis was a member of the famous Barker Gang. He was named Public Enemy Number One by J. Edgar Hoover, director of the Federal Bureau of Investigation. Karpis was a thorn in the side of the agency and Hoover harbored a real dislike for him. Karpis was born in Montreal, Canada in 1907, but spent his childhood in the state of Kansas. He was serving time for armed robbery when he met Freddie Barker. Through this acquaintance with Freddie, he was asked to join up with the notorious Doc and Ma Barker gang. In just a short time, they became known as the Karpis-Barker Gang.

It didn't take but a few months for the gang to make a name for themselves having robbed three banks in just the first month. They went from robbing banks to kidnaping. Their first victim was a St. Paul, Minnesota brewery millionaire. They held him in demand for a one hundred thousand dollar ransom. His family paid the ransom and he was released. This was in 1933, during the Great Depression when a dollar was a dollar.

Edward Bremer, a Minneapolis banker, was their second victim. They raised the ransom and received two hundred thousand dollars for Bremer's release. After this, the Karpis-Barker Gang was rich. However, in late 1934 F.B.I. agents captured Doc Barker. He stood trial and was sentenced to life in prison, and was sent to Alcatraz. He was shot to death in an attempted escape in 1939.

Doc's arrest didn't slow down the Karpis-Barker Gang though. In April 1935, they robbed a train netting them a score of thirty-four thousand dollars. The F.B.I. caught up with Ma and Freddie Barker in their hide-out in Florida in late 1935. They refused to surrender and died in a rain of bullets that completely destroyed the house where they were holed up. With the death of Ma and Freddie, and with Doc in prison, the Karpis-Barker Gang was at its end.

Karpis was hiding out in New Orleans in May 1936 when the F.B.I. found out where he was. The agents notified J. Edgar Hoover that they had Karpis cornered. Hoover boarded a plane and was there to take credit for Karpis' capture. Karpis was given a life sentence and shipped off to Alcatraz where he reunited with Doc Barker and two other members of the Karpis-Barker Gang.

In 1962 Karpis was transferred to the Federal Penitentiary at McNeil Island off the State of Washington.

In January 1969, after serving thirty-two years, Karpis was paroled. He was deported to Montreal and three years later he moved to Madrid, Spain. He died in 1979 at age 72.

Mickey Cohen,
West Coast Mafia Boss

Mickey Cohen was a very colorful individual. After his boss, Bugsy Siegel was killed by the Mafia, Mickey Cohen became the top dog on the West Coast. The Mafia was also after Mickey and he was in the news about every week. His home was bombed, and he and three of his associates were shot.

One of his bodyguards, Johnny Stompanato was stabbed to death by the daughter of the famous movie star, Lana Turner. Johnny and Lana had an off-on relationship for about a year. They were having a violent argument and Lana's daughter, Cheryl, 14 years old, overheard the argument. She feared for her mother's life and went to the kitchen and got a butcher knife. She rushed back to the bedroom where the argument was still going on, hot and heavy. She plunged the knife into Johnny's stomach. He bled to death within minutes. In court, a coroner's jury delivered a verdict of justifiable homicide.

Cohen hit Alcatraz thinking that his reputation and

money would get him some type of special treatment. His reputation as a crime boss did get him a couple of self-appointed bodyguards. An inmate by the name of Billy Boggs was a young tough who never bothered anyone. He celled next to Cohen and looked after Mickey's every need and made it known not to mess with Mickey or they would hear from him.

Cohen was serving fifteen years for tax evasion. When Alcatraz closed, he was transferred to the Federal Prison at Atlanta. While there, he was attacked by a con named Estes McDonald. McDonald hit him with an iron pipe. Cohen was transferred to the Federal Medical Center in Springfield, Missouri and was in a coma for eleven days. He recovered enough to get around with the use of a cane. After serving ten years, he was granted a parole in 1972. That was the last that I ever heard of him. He died in 1976 of natural causes.

Robert Stroud,
Bird Man of Alcatraz

The most famous inmate on the Rock when I arrived in 1959 was Robert Stroud, the Birdman of Alcatraz. At age 22, in 1909, Stroud was in the pimping business protecting an attractive blonde in Juneau, Alaska. A local bartender used the blonde's services and refused to pay her. She complained and the bartender beat her up pretty good. When Stroud found out, he was furious.He walked into the bar and shot the bartender dead. At trial, he was sentenced to a 12 year term in the Federal Penitentiary at McNeil Island. While there, in 1911, Stroud stabbed a prison stool-pigeon. This got six months added to his sentence and a transfer to the Federal Penitentiary at Leavenworth, Kansas.

In March of 1919, Stroud had a run-in with a guard in the mess hall. The guard started after Stroud and Stroud pulled a knife and stabbed the guard to death. At trial, he was given a death sentence. Stroud's mother wrote to President Woodrow Wilson pleading for her son's life. In April of 1920, just a few days before he was to be hanged, President Wilson commuted the sentence to life imprisonment. The powers that be were very unhappy and decided to extract their own measure of revenge, and Stroud was placed in solitary confinement for a period of what turned out to be a brutal thirty-nine years.

During the time spent in solitary, Stroud was permitted to raise canaries in his cell. Over the years he became an authority on bird diseases. He educated himself in the science of ornithology and wrote two books on the subject. He was very fond of his birds and when they became ill, he operated on some with the only tool that he had available, a razor blade, in an attempt to save their lives. Eventualy he had so many birds that he was running out of space to keep them. The warden of Leavenworth had the wall between his cell and the next removed, which increased Stroud's cell to double size. He now had plenty of room to continue his experiments with the birds.

Suddenly, however, things changed. A new warden took charge who believed in rigid enforcement of the rules. In December 1942, Stroud was informed that he was being transferred. Within the hour he was on his way to Alcatraz. Upon his arrival there, he was again placed in solitary confinement. They had prepared a special cell for him in the prison's hospital. In 1957 after fifteen years in this hospital cell, Warden Paul Madigan permitted Stroud to have yard privileges and allowed him to mingle with the other cons. He was still housed however, in the hospital cell.

He became very popular with the other cons and would sit on the large concrete bleachers talking with the inmates who gathered around him. Somehow, through the years he managed to keep a diary of the dismal life that he had suffered through. It was smuggled out and wound up in the hands of his attorney who found a publisher who put the diary into book form. It became a best seller and was made into a movie starring Burt Lancaster, *The Birdman of Alcatraz*.

Ironically, Stroud was never allowed to watch the movie depicting his life story. In 1959 his health was failing and he was transferred to the Federal Medical Center at Springfield, Missouri. Even then, being a frail old man, he was confined in one of the hospital's isolation ward cells. Robert Stroud died in 1963 at the age of 76.

D Block

The Isolation Ward, Segregation Unit, and the Treatment Unit are all names that are given to a section of a prison where rule breakers and unruly, tough-nut misfits are temporarily housed. Every prison in the United States, whether it be a State or a Federal institution, has a designated section for inmates who break the rules in some manner. Infraction of the rules can range from a very minor incident, to escape or attempted escape, to murder of another inmate or guard. The length of time the inmate serves in isolation depends on the type and seriousness of the infraction committed and the amount of information that the involved inmate is willing to give to the authorities. My personal experiences with time spent in different isolation units are not pleasant memories. My name for these units was always "the hole", because all of them were just that.

My first encounter was in the Iowa Training School for Boys, when I was caught smoking, which was against the rules, and I was sentenced to serve thirty days in segregation. The first ten days were spent in what was called "the box". The box was not big enough to enable one to sit up in it, or long enough to for one to lie down. You remained in a cramped position at all times. Using the bucket that served as the toilet was all but impossible. You were let out for ten minutes each morning to empty your bucket and wash yourself as best you could. It was not a very pleasant place. Food consisted of bread and water twice a day. The average weight loss for a thirty day stay was about twenty pounds.

For some unknown reason I never saw the hole while I was incarcerated by the California Youth Authority. The isolation unit at El Reno, Oklahoma was a barren cell with a steel bunk, one piece toilet and sink combined. The clothes that were given to us to wear consisted of a one-piece coverall. We were given no bedding at all during daylight hours, and at night, we were furnished with a dirty mattress and an army surplus blanket. Food was one-half rations and no desserts, twice a day. I spent three days in that hole for defending myself against five gang members who attacked me intending to take my possessions and to sexually assault me. They failed in their attempt and though I got a few bruises, those five guys knew that they had been in a fight. I was never bothered again after that.

I got a good taste of isolation in the Clark county jail in Las Vegas, Nevada after I and some others escaped from it. When we were captured, we were housed in the Las Vegas city jail's nut ward. However, the cells were really nice! They had nine mattresses, all hanging on the walls, or in plain words, a padded cell. I was held there until I went to the State Penitentiary at Carson City,

Nevada, and there I was housed in their lock-up unit which was a regular jail cell. I served ninety days in there before I was allowed in the general population.

My next encounter with isolation was in the Woodbury county jail in Sioux City, Iowa, when after another escape attempt I was given one of those nice cells with all the mattresses hanging on the walls. Actually, padded cells are not really that nice. There are no toilets or running water so you have to use a bucket. When you receive your meal, you also receive water and a clean pail. The lights are recessed into the ceiling and left on at all times. You also are not allowed to have any clothing and as a result you are cold all of the time.

At the Federal prison at Leavenworth, Kansas, I learned to what extent one could be at the mercy of the guards who had charge of us. I was arrested in the exercise yard one afternoon by three guards and taken to the "64 building", another name for the isolation ward. Some tools had come up missing from the plumbing shop where I happened to be assigned to work. I really did not know where the tools were or who had taken them. However, my record showed that I was involved in numerous escapes before I got to Leavenworth, plus I was serving a sentence of eighty years, reason enough to be suspected of wanting to escape again.

I spent the first night in the hole and the next morning I went before the Associate Warden. He asked me what I knew about the tools missing from the plumbing shop. I told him that I didn't know what he was talking about. He thought that I was lying to him and he tried to get me to change my story but as I truthfully didn't know anything, there was nothing I could do. He became very angry. That night when the guard shift changed, four officers opened my cell door and came in. They were all wearing baseball chest protectors, shin guards and face masks. One asked me if I wanted to tell them anything about the missing tools. Again I told them that I did not know what they were talking about, even though I knew that my answer was going to get me a good slapping around. I just didn't know how bad it was going to be.

They not only used their fists on me but when I fell down from the beating they all kicked me until I was nearly unconscious. I heard them laughing among themselves and I heard one of them say that I would have some answers for the Associate Warden in the morning. Of course I didn't have any answers for the A.W. the next morning but they had some more beating for me that night. In fact, I got a beating from them just about every other night for the next three weeks. After twenty-nine days of this treatment in the hole, they put me upstairs in the isolation ward. In about a month I was on my way to the Rock.

The Famous D Block of Alcatraz

The one and only time I was in D Block was not at all a very pleasant experience. Again I was to find out how completely at the mercy of the guards I was. I was caught carrying a knife and that infraction of the rules called for a thirty day stay in D Block.

I was put in one of the double-door cells on the main floor. When both doors were closed you were in complete darkness and completely naked. The toilet was a five inch hole in the floor. Your water source was a pipe sticking out of the back wall directly over the hole in the floor. You had to get the guard to turn on the water and that always became a game. They seemed to think that it was fun to tease you and turn the faucet just enough to produce a few drops of water. Dispensing toilet paper was another game they enjoyed, giving you three or four squares, never enough to really clean yourself.

With nothing to keep you warm, you were always cold and miserable. Food was half rations, twice a day. The only good thing about chow time was the warm coffee. I would rub the tin cup over my body absorbing the warmth. Of course that lasted only a few minutes but you can't imagine how good those few minutes felt.

The good thing about being in isolation was that I began to reflect, for the first time, about the life I had chosen and where it had gotten me. It was in the hole, naked and cold, that I began to talk to God, and first asked Him to help me. I know it sounds strange, but He answered me and I began to change.

I spent my twenty-nine days of misery and was sent back to the general population. I went back to work at my job in the kitchen. I was very careful after that not to be caught breaking any rules. Another stay in D Block I did not want.

Tomoya Kawakita

"The Jap" as he was referred to by all of the cons, was an American born Japanese. In fact he was born in El Centro, California. He went to Japan to study law and was there when the United States declared war on Japan. Kawakita was unable to return to the US so he took a job as an interpreter at a prisoner of war camp.

It seems that Kawakita was a sadist. He caused many American G.I.s to suffer savage beatings and as they screamed and begged for mercy, he took delight in their plight. Too weak and helpless to defend themselves, their pleas fell on deaf ears. Kawakita was wholly without mercy.

When the war ended, Kawakita returned to the United States. He was living in the Los Angeles area and one day he was recognized by an Army Sergeant who had suffered greatly at the hands of the Jap. The Sergeant's wife was with him as he pummeled the Jap unmercifully. She and other onlookers were shocked at the sudden and ferocious bare-fisted attack. When a police car pulled up, the officers took both the Sergeant and Kawakita off to jail. At the station, the Sergeant explained why he had attacked Kawakita. The police turned the matter over to the FBI and in just a short time the Sergeant was released.

Kawakita was charged with his war crimes and tried for treason. He was convicted and sentenced to death. Kawakita's attorney appealed the case for years and in 1954 President Eisenhower commuted his sentence to life behind bars. He would have been put to death in the gas chamber at San Quentin prison where he was being held. After his sentence was commuted he was transferred to Alcatraz.

Upon his arrival at Alcatraz, the warden knew that he had a problem on his hands., It would be a short lived time before someone killed the Jap. They assigned him to work in the hospital where they made a cell for him. He lived and stayed at all times in the hospital for several years. Finally he was given permission to go to the exercise yard if he so chose, but he was still to remain in his hospital room cell as opposed to living in a cell in general population.

Bored with being confined to the hospital, Kawakita decided that he would take a chance on the exercise yard. He took along several packs of cigarettes for bribes and headed out to the yard. Cigarettes were very scarce on the Rock. We were given three packs per week each, so cigarettes were always in demand. Heavy smokers were constantly bartering for extra smokes.

Kawakita thought that he had come up with a sure-fire way to make friends as he offered a cigarette or two to any con who approached him, as a goodwill gesture. Thanks to the prison grapevine all of the cons knew all about Kawakita and the atrocities that he had done to our soldiers during the war. No one would have anything to do with him. Whenever a con had a bad day, he would use the Jap for a punching bag. They tried several times to kill him, but somehow he survived. Finally they transferred him to some other prison and that was the last that I ever heard of him.

Attempt Escapes

Of the fourteen attempted escapes from Alcatraz, I have first hand knowledge of only two. I was on the island when the Anglin Brothers and Frank Morris left the dummies in their bunks and disappeared never to be heard from again. I was in the kitchen the night that Scott and Parker went out the window in the kitchen basement. Parker only made it to the rock known as little Alcatraz where he was picked up. Scott made it to the shore in San Francisco. There are other descriptions of these two attempts elsewhere in this book.

Following is a list of escape attempts from Alcatraz:

No. 1	Joseph Bowers	AZ 210, shot to death
No.2	Theodore Cole	AZ 258, drowned
	Ralph Roe	AZ 260, drowned
No.3	Thomas Limrick	AZ 263, shot to death
	Rufus Franklin	AZ 335, captured
	James Lucas,	AZ 224, captured
No. 4	Arthur (Doc) Barker	AZ 268, shot to death
	Dale Stamphill	AZ 435, captured
	Rufus McCain	AZ 267, captured
	Henri Young	AZ 244, captured
	William Martin	AZ 370, captured
No. 5	Joseph Kretzer	AZ 548, captured
	Arnold Kyle	AZ 547, captured
	Sam Shockley	AZ 462, captured
	Llloyd Barhdoll	AZ 423, captured
No. 6	John Bayless	AZ 466, captured
No. 7	Harold Brest	AZ 467, captured
	Floyd Hamilton	AZ 523, captured
	Freddie Hunter	AZ 402, captured
	James Boarman	AZ 571, shot to death
No. 8	Huron (Ted) Walters	AZ 536, captured
No. 9	John K. Giles	AZ 250, captured
No.10	Barnard Coy	AZ 415, shot to death
	Marvin Hubbard	AZ 645, shot to death
	Joseph Cretzer	AZ 548, shot to death
	Miran (Buddy) Thompson	AZ 729, captured
	Clarence (Joe) Carnes	AZ 714, captured
	Samuel Shockley	AZ 462, captured and executed

No. 11	Floyd P. Wilson,	captured
No. 12	Clyde Johnson,	captured
	Aaron Burgett,	drowned
No. 13	John Anglin,	unknown
	Clarence Anglin,	unknown
	Frank Lee Morris,	unknown
	Allen West,	captured
No. 14	John Paul Scott,	captured
	Daryl Parker,	captured